PAPI

PAPI

My Story

DAVID ORTIZ

with

MICHAEL HOLLEY

HOUGHTON MIFFLIN HARCOURT   BOSTON   NEW YORK

www.hmhco.com

Library of Congress Cataloging-in-Publication Data is available.
ISBN 978-0-544-81461-5

Book design by Brian Moore

Printed in the United States of America
DOC 10 9 8 7 6 5 4 3 2
4500657280

To Red Sox fans, my second family. Playing for and winning with you is one of the biggest thrills of my life.

— David Ortiz

For my lifelong advocates, Michelle and Aryl. I'm proud to be your brother.

— Michael Holley

Contents

PAPI

Introduction

For many reasons, the statistics say that I shouldn't be here.

I think about that all the time, even when I'm lounging on a beach with a nice drink in my hand. The thoughts carry me away, and I alternate between daydreams and remembrances of things that I was spared from. This was a time long before I was celebrated for baseball milestones and home runs in the bottom of the 9th, 10th, or even 12th inning. It was many years before I cursed terrorists and spoke up for freedom without fear. It was before I split my days between trying to win games for the Boston Red Sox and trying to save my sinking marriage, for the sake of my family. Yes, it was even before I became known by a nickname, Big Papi, that resonates throughout Boston, Santo Domingo, and anywhere in the baseball world.

The statistics then had nothing to do with my output as a designated hitter. No one, outside of my family, would have guessed that I would one day redefine the position and accumulate more home runs, hits, runs scored, and runs batted in than any DH in history. But to get there, celebrated and cheered by millions, I had to survive a neighborhood that didn't attract adoring crowds and the bright lights of television.

I grew up in Haina in the Dominican Republic. The city itself was recently cited as one of the most polluted places in the world. There was a battery recycling plant headquartered there, and as a result, battery acid and lead would seep into the soil. Piles of batteries, some as high as three-story buildings, could be found in the city. That alone put lives in danger. Then there was my neighborhood, which I made it out of by grace. My parents, Enrique and Angela, were strict on my younger sister, Albania, and me. They had to be. Our lives depended on it. We were poor, and our neighborhood was teeming with violence and crime. Shootings. Stabbings. Drugs. Gangs.

The statistics say I shouldn't be here.

My parents tried everything they could to protect us from our surroundings while we lived there, all the while hustling to make enough money so we could get out. Our house was small, with the main rooms divided by walls no thicker than plywood. That small house was large enough to have patches of land in the front and back, our yards, and the backyard was the only place where Albania and I could play in the neighborhood. The fear, from my mom and dad, was that we'd get caught in some crossfire that had nothing to do with us.

There are a few things from growing up that stay with me now, seared into my memories forever. I remember my parents sitting Albania and me down and showing us a bag. It had what appeared to be a white, powdery substance in it. I can still remember the stern looks on their faces, their eyes making contact with ours and locking there for the entire, brief warning.

"You will probably see this. Someone might ask you to take this. Don't do it."

The bag contained a type of cocaine that had been circulating through the neighborhood. My parents were concerned enough to physically show it to us so we would know exactly what to avoid. They also firmly delivered a message that I still share with young people today: drugs can be around you, and someone can offer you drugs . . . but there is nothing that says you have to take them. Nothing. Ultimately, you control the situation.

Some things were beyond controlling, beyond the shield and shelter of my parents. Once, my mother sent me to the bodega to pick up some groceries. On my way there, I saw a guy murdered. Right in front of my eyes, killed. I saw things that no one should see, especially a kid.

I saw it, yet never became it, thanks to God and my parents. To this day, I'm a ghetto boy who made it out, but where I came from still is in me. I don't let people see it, especially in the corporate circles I'm in now. Yet I never forget. If I ever do, that'll be the day that I lose my humility, so I'm glad to remember.

I'm glad that my three children have never had to live under the physical and financial pressures that I did as a kid. But in retrospect, my upbringing equipped me for every success and challenge I've ever had in baseball. Every single one. Watching my parents in that environment taught me about discipline, hard work, and being a provider, even amid the worst circumstances. I'd always laugh inside when I heard people talk about producing in the clutch in baseball. Please. That was nothing. I can tell you that I never felt pressure, not one time, strolling to the plate in a baseball game. I knew I wasn't going to get shot playing baseball. I knew that something I did could lead to a celebration, and I like to celebrate.

As adventurous as my life in baseball was over the course of twenty years, it was still a life *in baseball*. There were rules in place. Guidelines. In baseball, there were certain things that always could happen, or never could happen. My life, my real life, wasn't like that. And that unpredictability led to several life-changing events.

On the first day of 2002, I received news so devastating that I thought my heart would never fully recover. And I'm still not sure that it has. I learned how much sports can hurt people in 2003 and, in 2004, how they can help heal people too. I saw the goodness and beauty of an entire organization, singing together, in 2007. I had my character, my very essence, questioned and mocked in 2009. The next year I was urged to give up baseball and go home. Three years later, in 2013, I was the MVP of the World Series. In 2016, in the final regular-season game of my career, I looked to heaven for the spirit of my mother. My father was standing by my side. The president of the Dominican Republic was there. And on the field, cameras roamed and flashed, prepared to share my story with millions of people.

But that was just a small part of it. It all began in Haina, fighting against violence in the air and on the ground. That's where I, Enrique and Angela's son, learned to survive. They taught me how to work. The journey that followed taught me how to persevere and yet be transformed.

I find it amazing, and ironic, that a life beyond anything I've ever imagined has been made possible by playing baseball. I say that because baseball isn't even the sport I wanted to play.

Who didn't want to be like Mike in the late 1980s and early 1990s? I was a kid, and I played and thought about basketball constantly. My friends and I would go neighborhood to neighborhood, trying to find basketball games. I remember playing a tournament in Santa Rosa, about a 90-minute drive from my home in Haina. We knew all the NBA stars: Michael Jordan, Karl Malone, Magic Johnson, Charles Barkley, Larry Bird. I was big for my age, six feet tall when I was 10 and six-four at 14, and I was a power forward. Man, I was athletic, and I could run and jump. I thought it was the most beautiful game, exciting and entertaining, and that's what I wanted to do.

My father Enrique always had different plans. He was happy that I was interested in sports at all, since that made it less likely I'd be drawn into the chaotic environment of our neighborhood — people caught up in gangs, shootings and murders, people lost to drugs, in a big way. My country, unfortunately, became known as a Caribbean bridge for drug trafficking between the United States, South America, and Europe. There were billions of dollars in international drug transactions, which led to some dark, depressing, and corrupt tales in the Dominican. It had a devastating effect on the culture then, and it's still a huge problem now.

It was bad in my neighborhood, but things got a little rougher, emotionally, when my mother and father began to have a hard time in their relationship. My parents were already in the process of building a house together in Haina, in a community safer than the one we were in. But my folks were arguing a lot as the new house was being built, so they briefly separated before it was finished. My mother's sister had a big house, and we moved in with her for a while. My father wasn't officially living there, but he was so attentive that I don't ever remember feeling his absence. Once, he became angry when he heard that some people at my aunt's place looked at me, decided that I wasn't busy enough, and suggested it was time for me to go to work like every other adult in the house and start earning some money.

I was thirteen.

There was no way my father was going to let that happen. He wanted me to go to school, he wanted me to live with his sister . . . and he wanted me to play baseball. He played some ball in his day, as a pitcher, and whenever I talked to him about my love of basketball, he talked to me about the beauty of baseball. He insisted that I was going to be in the big leagues, and he'd always point out that my hand-eye coordination was exceptional. He was passionate about baseball, and now I understand that he wanted to see my excitement level for the game match my gift for it. I was tall and athletic, and my swing was whip-quick.

My father always bragged about me, how I had the size and strength to play in the big leagues one day. He was talking about me to a friend of his one day, and the friend asked me what position I liked to play. I told him first base. "Oh," I remember him saying. "It's going to be tough to make it there." I can understand now why he reacted that way. A lot of the best position players who made it from the Dominican to the majors were middle infielders and outfielders. You didn't see a lot of kids like me saying they were going to play first in the big leagues.

In every way possible, my father was always finding a way to encourage my appetite for baseball. He had a friend in the restaurant business who often traveled to New York City. My dad's friend used to go to a place in the city where Yankees first baseman Don Mattingly would have dinner. He approached Mattingly once and said, "I've got a friend in the Dominican. If you could sign something for him, he would die! Anything you can do." Mattingly surprised us all with something that became my trophy at home: he signed a bat, one he'd apparently gone 2-for-4 with. I've never told Mattingly that I was the kid he gave that bat to. But his generosity taught me a lesson. You never know how much inspiration you can give someone with a small gesture.

I can still remember the exact moment when I really fell for the game. I was about a month away from my 16th birthday, in the fall of 1991, and my father wanted me to watch the World Series with him. It was the Minnesota Twins and Atlanta Braves, and five of the seven games were decided by one run. Before that Series, honestly, watching baseball had been a little boring for me. When you watch the game now on TV, the camera angles and close-ups make you feel like you're actually at the game. It wasn't like that when I was growing up. But that Series changed everything. I couldn't take my eyes off of Kirby Puckett. He probably became my favorite player based on what he did in Game 6. With his team trailing three games to two, he was all over the field. I had never seen anything like it. He tripled in the first inning, climbed a 13-foot wall in the third to take away an extra-base hit, had a sacrifice fly in the fifth, singled in the eighth, and homered in the eleventh to win it and force Game 7.

Even after watching all of that, I can't truthfully say that I imagined myself winning late-night playoff games like Puckett did. "We'll see you tomorrow night," broadcaster Jack Buck said after the Puckett home run. Years later, Buck's son, Joe, would use a similar line when talking about me. My father may have envisioned all those things, but I didn't. It never crossed my mind that one day I'd dress in the same clubhouse, try to connect with the same fans in the Twin Cities, and play for the same manager as Hall of Famer Puckett (although I'm sure Kirby had a much better relationship with manager Tom Kelly than I did).

At 16, I was still too far away from the majors to have major league dreams. My father and a handful of local scouts said I was destined for the big leagues, but I wasn't sure of the path I was going to take. Because I was a first baseman with a rising swing, some people started calling me "the next Fred McGriff." The only thing I had in common with Fred McGriff at the time was that we were both tall lefties. He was in the middle of an impactful stretch of six consecutive 30–home run seasons. It was an honor to be in the same sentence as someone like him.

The Florida Marlins were on the verge of being an expansion team, and like everyone else in the majors, they were scouring the Dominican for talent. I was at their facility daily, and I seemed to be their only first baseman. I got a lot of work there, maybe too much work — I developed painful inflammation in my elbow. The Marlins sensed that I couldn't help them much, and they essentially kicked me out of camp and told me they might give me a look when I felt better.

I was heartbroken. Everything I had seen and done in baseball up to that point had been positive. I can't say that I'd ever had anything close to a setback before being cut by the Marlins. I was skilled and strong, and there wasn't any reason to think I couldn't do something. But then there was the pain of being cut.

The year before that, I had been casually hanging around the Mets' facility. I was facing pitchers much older than me, and I remember one of them throwing a fastball in the high 90s. I was young and raw, and the pitcher wasn't trying to fool me. He just wanted to prove to me that his unhittable fastball could handcuff me and any other 15-year-old who wanted to step into the box against him. But I kept spoiling his pitches. It was foul ball, foul ball, foul ball, over and over. The at-bat ended with me lining out to right field, but that performance would cause a buzz on the island. By the time I was in the Marlins' program, I was convinced they were going to sign me when I turned 17. Being sent home like that truly made me sick to my stomach.

My father saw me walk dejectedly into the house, and he noticed that I wasn't touching any food. I can still remember his words. "Son, what happened? Are you injured? Did you break a bone?" I told him what had happened, and it was the strangest thing — he let out a huge laugh. I said, "Dad, did you hear what I said? The Marlins let me go today." And he said, "I heard you. I'm laughing because they let go of a big league player today."

It's funny. The Marlins had just hired a new general manager to make the team competitive fast, and his name meant nothing to me at that time. Many years later, he'd become one of the few GMs who would seek my opinion on players and team-building. His name was Dave Dombrowski.

As I talked with my father, I mentioned that a man named Hector Alvarez had given me his business card as I was leaving Marlins camp. Alvarez was known as a *buscon* — someone who finds young baseball players and brings them to the attention of big league teams. The *buscones* have an important role, both for young players like I was and for major league teams. They are constantly mining for athletic gold on the island, and understandably so. In recent baseball seasons, as many as 10 percent of major leaguers have come from the

Dominican. So the talent is there, and the way the scouting system is set up, you could sign a dozen Dominican prospects and that would still be cheaper than signing a third- or fourth-round draft pick born in the United States.

Alvarez said he would train me, and the most important drill of his training program was common sense. That meant we did nothing, absolutely nothing, with my elbow. I rested it as I worked on other aspects of conditioning. I felt great, physically and spiritually. The dream that my parents had for me was still alive. The two of them couldn't have been better examples of how to carry on when a relationship goes south and there are kids involved. They couldn't figure out a way to be together anymore, but they never took that out on me and Albania. Looking back on it now, I have no idea how I did it, but I managed to stay in the middle. They were just Mom and Dad to me, and I loved them both. They showed me how to work too.

My mother was always taking on jobs to pick up extra money. She would sometimes travel to other parts of the Caribbean, as far away as Curaçao and St. Thomas, to buy clothes and sell them to tourists at local hotels. My father worked with all aspects of cars, from parts to repairs to sales. They worked hard so I could go to what is known as a *collegio,* as opposed to *escuela.* In the United States, that's the difference between a private school and a public school. The *collegio* was much better than the *escuela,* and a lot of my middle-class classmates there had no idea how far beneath them I was economically.

I never graduated from *collegio,* though, and with good reason: a week and a half after my 17th birthday, I signed with the Seattle Mariners. Four years after being spared from going to work, it was time to do it now. The days were long. I'd wake up at five, take the bus across town to get to the Mariners' facility at seven, stay there working and training until three, and then get back home around dinnertime. There was so much joy from my parents, who had worked so hard and made so many sacrifices just to get to that day. For years my father had guided me with the big leagues in mind. Consider that this is a man who, even now, speaks no English. He doesn't even say "Hi." But long before I signed with the Mariners, my father would tell me that I needed to learn English because I was going to need it at some point in my career. Truly, he saw a map for me when I was too young to see it for myself.

What I did know was that there was another center fielder in baseball besides Puckett who I needed to pay attention to — the Mariners' Ken Griffey Jr. When I watched him play, I thought that he was the Michael Jordan of the sport. He was so smooth, and he made it look easy. When I signed, Griffey was only 23 years old, yet he already had earned three Gold Gloves. He'd also earned a lot more than the $10,000 I signed for.

My parents got that money, bought me a nice stereo system so I could listen to my beloved music, and took the rest. They saved some of it, paid off some bills, and made a couple of purchases. That was it. Gone. It was a reminder of two critical things for me. One — and this is how I was raised — if you have something, give it to your parents. They had always supported me and done everything they could to make things better. The other thing? With the money arriving and departing so quickly, the message was clear.

I had to keep hustling.

1

The Desert

As soon as I got the phone call, I knew what was on my father's mind. He didn't spell it out for me, and I'm glad he didn't, because I understood what he wanted to hear.

"Que esta pasando?"

That's all he had to say — "what's going on?" — and the rest of the conversation was up to me. My father wanted to be assured that I wasn't going to quit baseball in the summer of 1994. He needed to know that I wasn't going to wither in the Arizona desert, as some of my teammates from the Dominican already had. I was 18 years old, away from home for the first time in my life, striving to get by with a limited understanding of English, and absolutely baking during our midday games in Peoria, a Phoenix suburb.

It was Rookie League baseball through and through, and if people couldn't see that they weren't paying attention. Our games were played in front of a few friends and family and a lot of empty seats. It was hard to blame anyone for staying away. It was always over 100 degrees when we played; most days it was about 105, but it wasn't unusual for the temperature to rise to 110 or 115. It was uncomfortable, but the heat was easy compared to everything else.

Listen, I didn't know anything — about life or baseball. When I left

Santo Domingo for Miami, and then Miami for Dallas, and finally Dallas for Phoenix, those were the first three planes I'd ever been on. I'd followed my father's advice and taken some English classes, but I quickly found out that the best way to learn the language is to screw it up and then be corrected by someone you trust. You can't take the corrections personally.

We all lived at a hotel, and I remember that there was a soda machine that we used. One of the new guys from the Dominican went there and tried to get a Coke. Keep in mind that it was one of those machines where you could put money in and it would tell you how much more was needed. My teammate was missing 10 cents. One dime. The word *dime* in Spanish means "tell me." He was putting his money in and saw the word DIME flash slowly in digitized red, so he asked us what it meant.

I explained that the machine wanted him to get closer and tell it the drink he wanted. Fortunately, he believed me. That led to at least 10 minutes of wild entertainment in the desert. He would say in a speaking voice, "Coca-Cola." And I would tell him that he wasn't being loud and clear enough. "Coca-Cola," he would say again, screaming this time.

On and on it went. We'd tell him to get louder. We'd tell him to switch the drink. We'd tell him to say it with authority. "Coca-Cola, dammit!" A few of us were dying laughing at this point, even as we continued to tell our friend that he was one good shout away from getting the soda of his choice.

Another time we had a teammate who couldn't wait an extra minute or two for us to go to McDonald's with him. Whenever I went there with guys from the Dominican, I was usually the translator. As rough as my English was, it was better than theirs. But my man was hungry, so he went ahead of us to get his chicken sandwich. The only problem for him was that he didn't know how to say "chicken sandwich" in English. We couldn't believe what we saw when we walked into McDonald's. He was basically playing charades at the register, flapping his arms like a chicken would, and then motioning to his mouth as if he were eating a sandwich. The cashier had no idea what he was saying and doing and gave him a puzzled look. But we knew. Once again, our laughter went on for a while. It was an adjustment period for everyone, and fun was one of the most universal ways to get through it.

The food there? Bland.

I was used to the rich, varied flavors of Dominican food. In Arizona, we'd get some plain scrambled eggs for breakfast and a piece of tough meat for dinner. We were young, but we were pro baseball players. We could just solve the problem and buy whatever we wanted to eat, right?

Not really.

Our pay was $118 every two weeks. We would have to make magic with that money and stretch $59 per week. You could go out at night, but doing that almost guaranteed that you'd be broke long before payday. We splurged a couple of times every two weeks. One of our treats was McDonald's, which was like America's Top Steakhouse to us. If it wasn't McDonald's, we'd go to a Chinese restaurant that featured an important phrase: "all you can eat." For $4.99, we could feast. We used to go in there and clean that place out.

I had some fun moments, but what stood out to me was that I had never felt so isolated before. I had been surrounded constantly by family at home, comforted by familiar sights, tastes, and smells, by the rhythmic pace of the island. The adjustment to American culture would have been challenging all by itself, but it also included playing pro baseball. All these new experiences combined could have been overwhelming, and that was one of the reasons my father was calling me. Another reason was that word had traveled quickly: people back home had learned that a few of my Dominican teammates decided that the march through the lowest level of the minors wasn't for them.

It could have been the food. It could have been the heat. It could have been the lack of guarantees and security. Some guys talked about venturing to New York, and others went back to the Dominican. For me, I remember it vividly. I was holding the phone, and I could hear that loaded question from my father. *Que esta pasando?* He was worried. He was nearly 3,000 miles away from me, but I could feel his concern, as if he were sitting right next to me. I was on my way to manhood after that conversation, because I was able to recognize the stakes and verbalize my plan.

"I'm staying," I told him. "I'm you guys' future, and I have one goal: make it to the big leagues. I'm strong. I'm not quitting."

I can't say that I heard him exhale, but I know that he did. He was agonizing over what I was going to say on that call.

Once we got past that hurdle, there was the business of actually playing baseball. This is going to sound strange to you, but I promise that it's true: I was so raw that I didn't yet understand some fundamental parts of the game. For example, I had no idea about batting averages. Isn't that crazy? Here I was, a professional baseball player, and I didn't understand the importance of batting .300. In fact, I didn't know anything about it my entire first year. I hit just a couple of home runs in about 50 games and hit around .250. It wasn't until the next season, as I overheard a coach talking, that I got it. The coach must have thought I was setting up a prank when I approached and asked, "So hitting .300 is a big deal in baseball?" He looked at me and said, "Of course!"

He saw that I was genuinely asking about it, so he explained it to me. Before that conversation, I had always had the mentality of having fun playing, doing what my coaches told me to do, and then trusting that anything after that would take care of itself. I guess they never came out and *told* me to hit over .300 and slug over .500. Now I had more of a plan. My second season in Arizona, I hit .332.

It was 1995 and I was just 19 years old. The star of the Mariners organization, Ken Griffey Jr., was in the majors by the time he was 19, but I knew that wasn't going to be my story. Griffey and his father were generous to me. They used to take care of the Latin players, bring us to nice restaurants, make sure we had good food. I was in awe of how real and earnest they were. Think about what they had combined to accomplish as a father-and-son baseball family and you come up with everything: World Series titles, All-Star Games, Gold Gloves, an MVP, millions of dollars. I respected them so much, and at 19, I was amazed that Junior had actually been in the majors at my age. I was admiring that accomplishment, not envying it, because I never dreamed of being in the big leagues that quickly. I was still learning the game as a young first baseman, and when I looked up —way up—at the guys playing my position in Seattle, I saw a pair of slugging Martinezes: Tino at first base and Edgar at designated hitter. The 1995 Mariners had no reason to obsess over impressive minor leaguers like me. Instead, they were charging toward the playoffs with hopes of making it to the World Series.

For me, I never imagined that my next stop, literally in a midwestern ghost town, would be my last full year in the minors. I was happy to finally be out of the desert, but it was as if my American education was going from one extreme to the other: from the excess heat of Arizona to the frequent chill of Wisconsin and the upper Midwest. My new team was the Wisconsin Timber Rattlers of the Midwest League. The stadium was in Grand Chute, officially listed as a ghost town; the major city in the area is Appleton.

It was the first time I'd ever seen snow. I remember looking around and wondering to no one in particular, "What is this? Do they really play baseball here?" The stadium was loaded with snow. They brought us players in to clear some of it away. Two days later, there was a huge snowstorm that canceled all the work we'd done.

I had five roommates, all Dominican, living in a two-bedroom apartment. Every time one of us made a phone call home, we'd put a clock in front of him to time it. It was an outrageous bill, and it was in my name. Another guy would have the cable, one would have the phone, and another the electric. That summer they disconnected the air conditioning unit, and it must have been the hottest summer ever. We'd share one fan. Take turns with it. Move it from one room to the next. It was inconvenient at the time, but those are the things that help me appreciate what I have now.

I was still translating for some of my teammates in Appleton, and the assignment was much more complicated. And rewarding, in a weird way. My teammate Dámaso Marté was dating an absolutely beautiful woman. They got along great and wanted to talk with each other often. But the problem was that Dámaso didn't speak English and she didn't speak Spanish. That's where I came in, to translate their conversations. Wherever they went, I would go as well. The only reason I did it was so my man Dámaso could be hooked up with a beautiful woman.

The manager of the team, Mike Goff, was someone who looked out for us. I remember him pulling some Latino and African American players to the side. He wanted us to be safe, and he wanted us to be mindful of the racist people he knew about in town. He told us to be aware of the Ku Klux Klan. He probably said that because of a situation that had happened before. Who knows? But I never saw anything racist in that town. Ever. Even going around the town, I never bumped into any racist situations. Goff had been the manager for years, though, and I guarantee that some situation had happened that he wanted us to be aware of. There's always some clown who pops up with something.

This guy took care of me, but he was hard on me. Goff would give me a fine for anything. He was intense, but one of our lighter moments together came following his ejection from a game. I thought he'd left the dugout and gone back to the clubhouse. Instead, he'd taken the mascot's uniform and was wearing it so he could remain on the field. Everyone knew the mascot was called "Thing." At one point I was lingering on the field and I heard Thing say, "Get your ass back in the dugout." When I heard Goff's voice, I understood what he'd done and started laughing.

Our team was close, so many of us lived and socialized together. One night a teammate wanted to meet up with some girls he knew at a club called the Fire Alarm. It was ladies' night, and it was $3 for all you could drink. I'd been paying attention to one of the girls. We talked, we joked, we played a couple of games of pool. I couldn't focus on anyone else, and I got the feeling that she didn't mind the attention I was giving her.

I found out that she was a local girl, from a small town called Kaukauna. She was a photography student in Madison and happened to be home for the weekend. I hadn't been drinking much, but whatever I did have must have been strong enough — enough to make me feel like I had Superman's cape on. When I saw the young woman dancing in a group, I moved across the floor and asked her a question.

"Do you have a boyfriend?" I said.

"No," she answered.

"Well, you do now," I replied.

She smiled. I knew right then I had something special with Tiffany Brick. She teased me for wearing what she described as a construction-site worker's outfit: long shorts and a bright-orange vest, with no shirt underneath. We danced the rest of the night. Eventually I learned how she spent the next day. She went to the local library and researched the Dominican Republic. She had a feeling that we would be spending a lot of time together, and she wanted to learn as much about me and my country as she could.

She was right about spending time together. Tiffany had been a great athlete in high school, voted Most Athletic Girl, and she still played fast-pitch softball. I would go to her games when I could and see her use her speed to get on base. When my team was on the road, she adjusted her schedule so she could see me. I met her parents, two brothers, and sister. She had never flown before, and we talked about her visiting the Dominican one day soon.

We had quickly fallen in love.

At one point during the summer, my roommates were having guests come in from Michigan, so our small apartment was overflowing and hot. Tiffany told me to stay at her house, although she was nervous about what her mother would say. I'd clicked with her mom when I'd met her before. When we woke up, we found out how Mom felt about me staying there for a couple of days: while we were sleeping, her mother had gotten on her bike, picked up some groceries, and returned to make a huge breakfast. It was obvious that Tiffany was going to be more than my girlfriend. I think we even mentioned the word "marriage" within the first two weeks of meeting each other.

I remember Tiffany asking what my other plan was if baseball didn't work out. I told her that my father was great with his hands, and that I came from a family of mechanics. Like my father, I was also great with my hands. My hands on the bat. I never had a thought that baseball wouldn't work out because I had confidence that it would. And to make life easier for my family, it had to.

2

Tom Kelly and Me

I had been doing something right on the field, because my season had been my best one yet as a pro. I was one of the top players in the league, hitting .322 with 32 doubles and 18 home runs. It felt good to have success, make a little bit more money — we were up to about $400 per week — and let my family know that I was getting a step closer to the dream.

At the end of the season, I found that I had made more money than I thought, and that I was closer to the majors than I thought.

The Timber Rattlers had made the playoffs. Goff called me into his office and handed me an envelope. It had all the fine money he had taken from me during the season. He gave it back to me.

"You know why I was so hard on you?" he asked. "Because you're going to be a major league baseball player. You gotta get your shit right before you get there. Good luck."

Our minor league season was over, but there was a full month of major league baseball to be played. I had done well in Wisconsin, but not to the point where I was thinking about having my name mentioned in the same sentence with a big leaguer. I was focused on getting back to the Dominican, training, and getting ready for my next challenge, most likely in Double A. But when I got back home, I received some news that filled me with pride.

I had been traded to the Minnesota Twins.

Some players are confused and unsettled by trades, but I wasn't. What stood out to me was that an established power hitter in the big leagues, third baseman Dave Hollins, had been traded straight-up for me, a kid in A ball. It built up my confidence. I was glad that Minnesota thought that highly of me.

At the time, I didn't have a handle on who the Twins were and what was systematically happening to them. Kirby Puckett had put the Twins on the map for me, but he wasn't going to be a teammate of mine. About six weeks before I was traded, Puckett announced his retirement after playing 12 seasons with Minnesota. He had developed glaucoma in his right eye, and his career was abruptly over at the age of 36. The Twins from that 1991 World Series I watched were not the Twins I was going to in 1996. The team had a winning record in 1992, but then followed that season with four consecutive losing ones. The team's front office was told to cut payroll, which made it possible for a lot of young and cheap players to get to the big leagues.

That was the good news for me, and I was excited about it. The Twins wanted to see what they had traded for, so it wasn't long before they brought me to the Instructional League in Fort Myers, Florida, and watched me take batting practice. Shortly after that, they put me on their 40-man roster. In spite of all these positive developments, though, it wasn't all positive.

Many things about the Twins had changed over the years, but the same manager was still in place. His name was Tom Kelly, and he was highly respected in the Twin Cities and throughout baseball. It didn't take me long to figure out that he was the kind of guy who could make your life miserable if he didn't like you. It also didn't take me long to figure out that he didn't like me. At all. This was going to require some problem-solving skills. This was going to be my biggest challenge yet in professional baseball.

In the spring of 1997, I was 21 years old. I had completed just one full season of minor league baseball. I was still learning the nuances of the game as well as the United States of America. So, no, I never expected to be in the major leagues that season. And I never dreamed that I'd have as many problems with a manager over the years as I did with Tom Kelly.

Anyone who was around the Twins knew that Kelly had never wanted to move on from Dave Hollins, the player I was traded for. Hollins was a veteran player, and maybe his departure showed the manager his own future in Minnesota: managing with fewer and fewer veteran players on the roster the longer he hung around. I can imagine it must have been frustrating for a two-time World Series–winning manager to see his team brought to its knees by age, trades, and cost-cutting.

I wasn't thinking about any of those issues, though, when I showed up for spring training. I just wanted to hit and prove that I was ready to move on from A ball. I was crushing the ball that spring, and I can remember the Twins' Double A manager, Al Newman, telling me, "I wish I could take you with me. You belong in Double A." He said that because I wasn't going with him, and I wasn't happy about it. The Twins trained in Fort Myers, and I was staying right there. My hot spring had earned me a slight promotion, from Low A the year before in Wisconsin to High A and the Fort Myers Miracle in the Florida State League.

I still had a lot to learn, but I wanted to be challenged too. I knew my skills were beyond that league. It took a couple of months for the Twins to agree with me. That's when the organization put me where I should have been all along: in Double A in New Britain, Connecticut.

As I look back now, it's clear how much tension there always seemed to be with the Twins: I saw myself as one kind of player and they usually had ideas different from mine. It wasn't all bad, though, because of the relationships I had with my teammates and with members of other teams. That year I got to play with my boys Torii Hunter, Corey Koskie, Doug Mientkiewicz, and Javier Valentín, guys who remain friends of mine.

As for other teams, Akron had a first baseman named Sean Casey who was probably the friendliest player in the league. I'd get to first base and he'd want to talk baseball, the weather, pop culture, or anything that crossed his mind. It's no wonder that he eventually became known as "the Mayor." When we played in Portland, Maine, another player I looked for was Kevin Millar. He was a good hitter, but more than that, he usually said something that made me laugh. It was tough to dislike a personality like that. I was growing, and these were the players I was growing up with. And the growth was happening fast.

My first couple of games in Double A, I was hitless. Newman approached me on the team bus with a smile. "It's not that easy hitting at this level, is it?" he said. It wasn't in the beginning, but I quickly adjusted in the next two months. I averaged an extra-base hit every seven at-bats, led the team with a .585 slugging percentage, and earned my second promotion of the summer. I was on my way to Salt Lake City and Triple A. Just one phone call away from the big leagues. While I hadn't thought of the highest level in the spring, it was within reach now. The Twins were having yet another losing season, one of the five worst teams in all of baseball. There wasn't anyone on the roster known for being a power hitter. The team leaders in home runs were Marty Cordova and Matt Lawton, with 15 and 14.

I was a September call-up on a bad team, and there were no big plans for me in 1997. But since I had risen so fast through the system, and since there wasn't another power hitter like me in the organization, I figured I would be sticking around for a while. It's hard to believe that it happened so fast: three years after my first trip to the United States, and one year since being traded as a prospect in A ball, I was officially a major leaguer. I liked my chances in 1998.

The Twins, though, and everyone else in Minnesota, had other things on their minds. Such as survival. The team's owner, a banker named Carl Pohldad, was upset that he couldn't get political support for a new retractable-roof stadium. He made it no secret that he was negotiating to sell the team to a businessman who planned to move the team to North Carolina.

As the '98 season began, that was the big question in Minnesota and throughout baseball: Is this the last year of the Minnesota Twins? The combination of the uncertainty, the losing, and the worst attendance in the entire American League made for a low-energy atmosphere. I could understand why they wanted a new stadium. The Metrodome was boring. It was nothing like the excitement I had seen as a kid when I fell in love watching Kirby Puckett.

Playing for Kelly made it even more miserable.

I know he's recognized as a good baseball man, but he struck me as a guy who believed his players were dumb fucks. I'll give you an example. The Metrodome was known for being a tough place to track the ball, as well as for its fast, unpredictable turf. You could be working hard, concentrating hard, and embarrassing things still could happen to you on the field. There was a game where Kelly thought the team was too sloppy, so he ordered the players onto the field after the game. Come on. It's major league baseball. I'd never seen anyone do that before, and I haven't seen anyone do it since. He didn't do well with mistakes, and there were lots of mistakes as our team gradually got younger. I walked on eggshells around him. I didn't like playing the way he wanted me to play. He loved those Punch and Judy, spray-the-ball-all-over-the-field hitters. He absolutely loved that kind of stuff. I'm not going to be putting the ball on the turf and moving runners over. I'm a big, left-handed power hitter who is supposed to drive in runs. That was my approach.

The approach seemed to be working fine the first month of the 1998 season. I hit four home runs and drove in 20 in our first 34 games, and I also led our team in slugging percentage. I felt great. I even got a compliment from Kelly, who told the people covering the team that I brought "pizazz" to the game. Unfortunately, I hurt my right wrist in a game against Tampa and broke it a week later in New York. I missed three months just as the weather was changing, when I believed I was going to become even more productive. Not only did the injury affect my season, as I finished the year with just nine home runs, but it made a shaky relationship with Kelly even worse.

I couldn't believe what happened the next year in spring training. The only significant thing that had changed in Minnesota was that the team was staying. There wasn't a new stadium in the works at that time, but at least Charlotte wasn't gaining the Twins. So it was back to the Metrodome again for yet another season of the worst attendance in the league. On the field, the team was even younger than the year before. Every single pitcher who started a game was in his twenties. Not one start, all year, from anyone over 30. Isn't that amazing? Anyway, the lineup featured some of my boys, like Torii Hunter and Todd Walker. Matt Lawton and Marty Cordova were there too, along with Ron Coomer, but for the third year in a row there wasn't an everyday player who slugged .500 or better.

You might be wondering why I wasn't that guy. Me too. This was a team desperately in need of, to use Kelly's word, pizazz. Yet, at the end of spring training, the Twins sent me to Triple A. When I'd made it from A ball to the big leagues in 1997, I thought my minor league days were over. Two years later, even after my wrist injury, it was clear to everyone that I was a 23-year-old hitter who belonged in the big leagues.

The Twins disagreed. I was one of the first cuts, and they used a poor batting average in spring training against me. I still get angry about it to this day. I put it all on Kelly. I think about his mentality at the time, and the games that he played with me. If I were of a lesser mind, if I didn't possess the inner strength that I have, it could have broken me. And just being very honest, it rocked me a bit. The message the organization was sending me was that I wasn't worth shit. I'd hit .277 for them the year before, with a hand that never fully healed, and they quickly sent me down like that? After I was supposed to be part of the organization's future? Way to build up my confidence, sending me down after a handful of at-bats in the spring.

As bad as that was, that wasn't even the worst of it. While I was in Triple A, my teammates and opposing players would look at me and say, "What in the hell are you doing here? You're a big leaguer playing the year in Triple A." My girlfriend Tiffany essentially kept a bag packed for me, ready for a grab-and-go at any time. She shopped day to day, rather than week to week, because she was always expecting me to get the call. We lived in the same apartment complex where many of my teammates lived, and their wives and girlfriends would tell Tiffany that they too thought I would be leaving soon. My numbers said it all: 68 extra-base hits, 110 runs batted in, and a slugging percentage just under .600 in 130 games. Remember, the big league team still had no power hitters. Yet the Twins left me in Salt Lake City the entire season. I even started to hear that the decision-makers in Minnesota were saying that I was dogging it in Triple A. It was so insulting. I don't know if those reports were coming from scouts or from Phil Roof, my Triple A manager, but if they thought that I was dogging it, what did they expect my numbers to be with "effort"?

My opinion of the organization was probably sealed at the end of the '99 season. My team in Salt Lake had made the Pacific Coast League playoffs. The Twins hadn't come close to calling me up all year, and they still didn't do it on September 1. I thought, naturally, that I wasn't going to the big leagues at all, so I put everything I had into our Triple A playoff series against Edmonton. Maybe I took it too far: caught in the scramble of a rundown, I injured the ACL in my left knee as well as my left ankle.

According to the trainers, I needed surgery and my season was over. But I was our best hitter, and we were in the playoffs. I went back to the hotel, took some anti-inflammatories, and told Phil Roof that I was available for the next game. Despite hitting a couple of homers on a bad leg, I didn't have enough to carry the team in that series. We lost, and I thought I had plenty of time to get myself together in the off-season because my baseball season was over.

Except that it wasn't.

After ignoring me the entire spring and summer, the Twins called me up when I was at my most vulnerable and ineffective. I was shocked. What were they thinking? I knew I was hurt, my Triple A manager knew, and so did everyone in Minnesota. When they called me up, I spent the next couple of weeks doing nothing but therapy. I didn't take batting practice, I didn't run the bases, I did nothing. Just therapy. One day the trainer saw me running in the outfield and determined that I was well enough to play. So, sure enough, Kelly put me into a game. My season should have been over. I was at a disadvantage, and it showed in my 25 at-bats. I didn't get a hit. Not one. Five walks, zero hits.

Sending me down for the year, calling me up when I was hurt, and then actually playing me while I was hurt — those were all low blows. It was as if they were saying, *Fuck you, man.* It was a real doghouse, and I didn't appreciate it. There was no use protesting. Kelly wasn't going anywhere, even after his seventh consecutive losing season. No one knew just how talented we were as young guys, so people didn't hold his record against him. Besides, he was a link to the past, the man who had guided the Twins to the only championships in franchise history.

I had a decision to make. I could fight Kelly, or I could learn to make him happy. So I kissed his ass for a couple of years and became the biggest slap hitter you'll ever see. Even that wasn't enough, not entirely. He never fully embraced me by entrusting me with either the first base or designated hitter job and saying, "Figure it out." No, I was always splitting the job with someone. It was tough because these were friends of mine and I had nothing against them. The problem was with Kelly. He once made a comment about me — essentially that they didn't know what to do with me and that no one wanted me. That was interesting to hear. One off-season in the Dominican, I saw Felipe Alou. He told me that his franchise, the Montreal Expos, had made calls about me, but the Twins weren't going to trade me.

So what were they trying to do? Maybe it was their attempt to humble me or prove to me that I couldn't do anything without them. As long as Kelly stayed there, I was never going to be the player that I should have been, coming into my prime years. He saw me as a part-timer. I saw myself as a player who needed to be included in the lineup daily, no matter who was on the mound. Since I wasn't writing out the lineups, I was a part-timer in 2000, when the Twins had their eighth straight losing season. I was also a part-timer in 2001, the season that broke a couple of strongholds.

First, it snapped the parade of losing, as the Twins finished with an 85-win regular season. It also ended the 15-year reign of "TK," which is what a lot of baseball people called Kelly. He retired to much praise at the conclusion of the 2001 season. The Twins were all that I knew in major league baseball, so I had no evidence to support my thought that there had to be something better than what I had experienced. I was hopeful, but I really didn't know.

I did know that I was going to be more free in 2002. No more acting like a singles hitter. No more unreasonable stays in the minors. No more Tom Kelly. My new manager was Ron Gardenhire, and I got the feeling that no matter what kind of leader he turned out to be, he was going to be better for me than Kelly was. It couldn't possibly be worse.

I knew it was going to be a year of great change for me in baseball, a change that would alter the way other people looked at me, as well as the way I looked at myself. I couldn't have imagined that the change would be so deep, beyond the game, affecting me more than a game ever could. I was young, but I'd seen a lot in my life. Yet, in 2002, it was one of the few times I could feel myself crumbling as I thought, *I can't believe this is happening.*

3

Crossroads

My favorite part of every baseball off-season was returning to the Dominican to see my mother Angela. I adored her and tried to do everything she asked. If I had plans to go out with my boys and my mom said, "Son, I don't want you to go," then I'd stay home. That was the relationship.

I respected all the things she and my father had done to make sure my sister and I had a decent life, so I wanted to repay that love every chance I got. At Christmas, we were always together as a family. My mother was a phenomenal cook, and I think she passed those genes on to me. I'm telling you, anything that she put her hands on was money. Rice, beef, chicken, fish. It was all good, and I'd often be there watching her make it. Christmas was when sisters and cousins and even neighbors would come by. They were full of love and laughter, and they'd make amazing meals that would take your speech and breath away, meals that let you know just how much they cared. There would also be music, dancing, and talking for hours and hours.

I loved it, and it was a reminder that no matter what had happened in the 2001 season, or any season, I had dozens of people who supported and loved me unconditionally.

I was 26 in the winter of 2001, Tiffany and I had been together five years and had two girls, and I had my own place in the Dominican. But that never stopped me from visiting with my mother, and even staying over if that was what she wanted me to do. I'd usually go to her house dressed casually, either in jeans or shorts. But something different came over me before I went to see her on New Year's Eve, December 31, 2001. I'd never suited up to hang out at Mom's house, but there I was, standing in front of my closet, pulling out and holding up suits to decide which one I'd wear that day.

The blue one came out first. Then the gray. Then the pinstripes. I went through a lot of options and colors, not even thinking about what I was doing. I finally settled on a black one. I put on a white shirt, a tie, and that black suit and drove to my mother's house. When she saw me, she smiled and raised her eyebrows.

"Damn, boy," she said. "What's up with this suit thing?"

"You know, Mom. I just want to look good for you," I said.

There was something different about the night, and I wasn't sure what it was. I was quiet inside. I love my music, loud and happy music, and my mom knew that. I'd go there and put it on, turn it up, play it for hours. But when my mother asked me if I was going to play anything, I told her I wasn't up for it. Her place had two levels, with a living room and kitchen downstairs and all the bedrooms on the second floor. Around nine o'clock at night, I went to take a nap in one of the bedrooms. That was strange, because I'd never done that either.

The way things were developing, and the way I was feeling, I should have known that life as I knew it was about to be altered forever.

When I woke up from the nap, the first thing I saw was a jersey that belonged to me, hanging in the closet. It was a Minnesota Vikings game-day model, number 84. For Randy Moss. I'd picked one up after his first year with the Vikings. Seeing it made me smile, because that was a great example of my mother's style. She was a tall woman who, even at the age of 46, had a little hip-hop swagger to her.

She liked to wear some of my things, and she was proud that her son was a professional athlete.

I'll never forget the dinner we had that night. The food was perfect, as it usually was, but the atmosphere wasn't as festive as normal. A couple of friends of mine had asked me to stop by a party they were going to, and I'd initially agreed to do it. I said good-bye to my mother, drove away from the house, and went all the way to the party. But when I was steps away from the entrance to the place, I decided I didn't want to go in.

Everything I did that night was different, and I was more subdued than anyone who knew me had been used to seeing. I didn't mistake that restraint for maturity, the idea that I'd suddenly grown up and lost my appetite for all the fun things I usually did. That wasn't it. Something was troubling me, and at the time I didn't know what it was.

I eventually got back to my own place, slept there, and called my mother on New Year's Day 2002. She said she was planning to call a driver she knew so he could take her to visit her brothers and sisters. My sister and I found out later that the driver first declined to take her. He had worked an overnight shift and said he was too tired to make the trip. Thirty minutes later, because of his love for her, he called back and said he couldn't tell her no.

That's how everyone felt about my mother. She had a lot of charisma; people were drawn to her personality. She connected with people easily too. If she knew you for 15 minutes and you told her you had a problem, she would immediately help you solve it, as if she'd known you all your life. It was difficult for anyone to leave her stranded when she was in need, so the driver and my mother took that drive across the island to see her family.

As she was visiting her brothers and sisters, I was at my own house, talking with my father. Some of my friends wanted me to go to the beach, where a lot of people would go on New Year's Day. I wasn't up to it. Later in the day, I drove my father back to his own house. I can remember every detail of sitting there, talking to my father, and having our conversation interrupted by a phone call. It was from a guy named Carlos, who was dating my sister at the time.

Carlos said he had been driving on the highway and had seen a terrible accident. He told me where it was and said I should get there quickly. I can still hear his voice now, how he had too much respect for me and my family to tell me what he already knew. He tried to be gentle. "Angela had an accident," he said, "and she's not looking too good."

He didn't want to tell me. He knew that she was dead. He just wanted me to get there.

The location he told me was about 20 minutes away from my father's house. My dad heard the entire conversation, so we sped away from his house and toward the location that Carlos described. We got there in about seven minutes, saw the wreckage, and were told what had happened. The driver had fallen asleep on the way home. My mother had been asleep as well, sitting in the backseat of the car on the right side. There was a dump truck parked on the side of the highway, and they ran into it. The driver was in critical condition and almost died. My mother died instantly.

A huge part of me was gone, taken away from me so suddenly that it did not seem real. I was shattered, and I have no idea how I even found the strength to stand through it all. I remember everything, step by step, like it happened yesterday. I'll tell you something that my sister and I still talk about to this day: When it was time to identify my mother's body, which was unrecognizable in so many ways, do you know how we knew it was her? She was wearing my Vikings jersey, the one I had seen hanging in the closet. We still talk about that now. We can look back and see all the mysterious things that happened over those couple of days. She'd insisted on that trip to see her family, and that had been her good-bye to them. My good-bye had happened the night before, wearing that black suit in sadness.

I trust God, and I know that He worked with me and my family during our mourning. We were all trying to stand up without someone who had been such a pillar for us, so important to so many people. My mom was the youngest of all her brothers and sisters, and the one who had looked out for her the most was my uncle. He was much older than she was, and he had been given instructions by their own mother many years earlier. She died when my mom was eight, and before she passed she told my uncle, "You have to raise *La Nina* now. I'll be watching."

La Nina. The little girl. That's how my uncle saw my mother. It wasn't a typical brother-sister relationship. He would check on her every Sunday and spend all day at her house. I remember my uncle at the funeral, looking up to the sky and crying, "Why her?" His son, my cousin, had died two years earlier in a bad jet skiing accident. He was still struggling from that, and then there was the death of my mother.

I looked around at the funeral and saw so many people who loved her, and were so heartbroken by her passing, that I instinctively felt that I had to be the strong one and couldn't grieve. I could feel my aunts and uncles leaning on me, looking to me for direction. Somehow I was able to give the appearance that I was keeping it all together, but I wasn't the same. I kept thinking that none of this was real.

It started to hit me after winter ball, when I began to get ready for my last spring training with the Twins. My mother was a part of my spring routines. She would always drive me to the airport as I left for the States. And then she would come to Fort Myers to celebrate her birthday, March 4. There would always be cake, and my teammates and I would give her a lot of attention.

But on March 4, 2002, she wasn't there. That was my first real struggle — accepting that she was not coming back. I'd kept so much to myself, working so hard to be contained for other people, but I couldn't do it anymore. I lost it.

One day I was walking slowly, alone, probably in a fog without knowing it. I missed my mother so much. Her goodness. Her advice. Her cooking. Her smile. Her mere presence. When I found myself standing alone in the Twins' parking lot, the memories overwhelmed me and I started bawling. I didn't know who saw me, and it didn't matter because I couldn't stop crying. My mother, my heart, was gone. Those tears had been stored up for months, since New Year's Day, and I was finally allowing them to be released.

One of the groundskeepers must have seen me and told my teammates. I looked up and saw Torii Hunter and others, coming out to hug and support me. Torii had been there at all of those birthday parties with my mother, and he understood her impact on my life. All I could do, going forward, was honor her with my work. I decided that every one of my home runs would be capped off with me pointing to heaven in remembrance of Angela, because I know that's where she is now.

Despite what happened with the Twins' decision-makers, what I valued most about our team was the relationships. We were a bunch of kids, we'd been promoted together in the minors, and we were having fun. We also cared about one another. That was one of the reasons I felt lucky to know these guys, because I knew that our relationships would carry us beyond baseball.

The season began just as we expected. We were a good team, so we won 13 of our first 19 games. I was slugging well over .500 with four April home runs. And then it happened. Again. This time it was an injury to my left knee, an injury that was going to require surgery and lead me back to the disabled list. Yes, things were turning around for the team, but not so much for me. Once again, I was going to need to regain the momentum I'd lost after being out for close to a month. I knew I could hit, but I could feel the organization beginning to wonder if I would ever be able to put together a complete and productive season.

The good news was that the team kept winning while I was gone, and we won after I returned. It took me nearly two months to recapture my hot start, but once I did my average climbed from .237 on July 1 to .282 on August 1. I'll tell you what else happened in that month: we started to run away with the division. No one was even close to us. On August 1, we led the division by 15 games, and by the end of the year we were the division champs, 20 games ahead of Cleveland and 13 ahead of the second-place Chicago White Sox.

It felt great to be going to the playoffs, with players I loved. It was the first time in my career that I'd finished with 20 home runs, and my on-base plus slugging percentage (OPS) was .839. My boys Torii Hunter and Jacque Jones had 29 and 27 home runs. Think about those years when the Twins' home run leaders were in the midteens; now we had three players with at least 20. We started to bring some people back to the park too. Our attendance wasn't great, but we also weren't last in the league in that category anymore.

But there was a problem, beyond losing the American League Championship Series to the Angels in five games. The problem was that the Twins still were not big spenders, and they had a lot of decisions to make. They were going to have to either pay me $2 million, trade me, or release me. That seems crazy to say now, with all the money in baseball and the sacrifices teams make to acquire power hitters. Today there isn't one team in baseball that would release a slugger rather than pay him a couple of million dollars. It was a different time in baseball back then. It was the steroid era, and many teams believed that there were many ways to find a guy who could give them 20 home runs.

I knew I was more than that, though. I got those 20 without 500 at-bats. If I ever got a chance to play every day, I knew I could do much more. That was the issue for Gardenhire and Twins general manager Terry Ryan. Were they willing to commit to me as a full-time player, at the age of 27, and use part of the limited budget to pay me? Their answer was a firm no. They called around and tried to trade me. They didn't get what they were looking for. So as I tried to enjoy the off-season in the Dominican, I got the news from my agent.

I was released.

That was it. I was no longer a Twin, no longer guaranteed to be teammates with the players I had lived with in the minors and the majors. It was a strange feeling. I knew I was going to find a job somewhere else, but I was devastated. It was like being separated from my brothers. The extremes we'd been through made it emotional for me. It's one thing to leave a winning team, but it's even worse when you leave a winning team after experiencing the depths of losing with them too. We'd been through a lot. We'd had a lot of good times at home and on the road, laughing, going out to eat, catching each other in practical jokes.

It was a hard reality to accept: I was now a guy who had been released by an organization, and not because I sucked. I was released because they didn't have the balls to pay me. Two million dollars was nothing for them. And yet they decided to let me go. I believed that I was a talented player who was about to break out. The Twins didn't want to go through that process with me. Instead, they replaced me on the roster with a player named José Morban. He was a shortstop they got in the Rule 5 draft, a player who had never competed above High A ball in the minors. Yet Ron Gardenhire told the *Minneapolis Star Tribune*: "He sounds like a hell of a player. From talking with all of our people, they were really excited and hoping we could get this kid." They picked him over me, simple as that. What I needed to find was some team that would see past the injuries and focus on what I could bring to a team and its clubhouse.

I still remember the petty incidents. Once, after the 1998 season, Gardenhire said his good-byes to players and staff and then came to me and said, "See you next year . . . if you're still here." I was like, damn. He probably doesn't remember that, but I do. I don't forget things. All I know is that the following year I was working on my timing in spring training and, in a ridiculous move, they sent me down to Salt Lake City.

I remember the silly stuff they used to do with my family. I had been with Tiffany for six years, and we had a life together. We weren't married, though, and the organization seemed to view that as less-than somehow. We were parents, we loved each other, and we were around each other constantly, but I guess that didn't matter to them without the marriage license.

There had been lots of trade rumors about me after the World Series and into early November. I was even thinking about those rumors on one of the best days of my life, November 16, 2002. On a rainy Saturday afternoon, on Fort Myers Beach, Tiffany and I finally did get married. We'd talked about being together for life within our first two weeks of being together, and now we were making it official. Many of my Twins teammates were there, and I remember emotionally telling Corey Koskie, "I think I'm going to be playing somewhere else in 2003."

Even though I'd said it, I wasn't prepared for it. The way I imagined it happening was all wrong too. As November became December, I'd go over scenarios on how it would happen. There would be a phone call, I thought, telling me I'd been traded to Miami or Chicago or New York. Yes, I thought I'd be traded. Not released.

I feel like they fucked me. That's the best way I can describe it. I was released on December 16, 2002, exactly one month after my wedding. Who gets released then? It was a difficult time to find a job, which is why I'd said to Terry Ryan during the season, "If you're going to release me, please just do it right after the playoffs."

I was good to that organization. I was one of the players who kept the clubhouse loose. I approached my teammates with humility, and I was loved by everyone. Why release me in December? I thought it was a trashy way to do business, and I couldn't help thinking that they'd done it on purpose.

When I got the news, I was in the Dominican. One of the first calls I made was to Tiffany. Our daughter Alex wasn't quite two years old, and now we had no idea where we'd be in 2003. But Tiffany can be a smart-ass at times. When I called her at her mother's house in Wisconsin and told her what had happened, she said, "Good. Now we can apply for a job in Boston."

She loved the city and Fenway Park, although one time she commented that a parking space in Boston costs roughly the same as a house in Minnesota. I told her that there were no job applications in baseball, which she already knew, but that Boston was a possibility.

One of the reasons it was an option was because of my friend Pedro Martínez. We had the same agent, and we'd been introduced to each other years earlier. We'd had lunch, and I was impressed by Pedro's recall and thoughtfulness. He said that as a pitcher he always kept track of players who were becoming hitting threats, and that I was on his list.

Nothing slipped by Pedro. I'd always hear from him about one item or another. Once he told me that he couldn't believe I'd hit a homer off him in Minnesota. He said he'd thrown me a cutter and that I was the only tall man he knew in baseball who didn't need to extend his hands to pull the ball. He explained that tall guys, power guys, want to extend their hands and pull it. He said he liked that I had been able to bring my hands in and pull it. He said that was special.

He had lots of opinions on the game. As a fellow big leaguer from the Dominican, he had a theory that most Latin players could hit fastballs because the constant challenges present in winter ball exposed them to so many fastballs. I was always fascinated by his detailed analysis of the game.

Shortly after my release, I was sitting in a restaurant in the Dominican with some friends of mine. Pedro saw me and said, "*Compa* [buddy], come eat with us." I was on the phone, so I put my hand up as if to say wait a second. I guess I was on the call longer than Pedro expected, so he came over and asked what was going on. I told him I'd been released by the Twins. I'll never forget his response.

"That's great," he said, with that big smile of his.

I made a face at him. Good? How so? I'd just gotten married and had a family to support, and now I had no job.

"No, no," Pedro clarified. "I'm saying it's great because now you get a chance to play with me in Boston."

Once Pedro put his mind to something, nothing else got in the way. From afar, the Red Sox appeared to be a bold team. I knew they had a lot of money to spend, and I didn't see anyone on their roster I couldn't beat out for a job. Pedro started making calls like he was a general manager trying to make a deal. He called the new general manager, 28-year-old Theo Epstein. He also repeatedly reached out to Larry Lucchino, the team president. He left messages with them that all ended the same way: "Please call me back." He got tired of waiting and contacted Jack McCormick, the traveling secretary. He got McCormick on the phone and said the words that certainly didn't hurt my cause: "I'm sorry to be disturbing you this time of night, Jack. I need to get ahold of Theo. Get this message to him: David Ortiz got released and he can be our new first baseman."

It had a chance to be a really good fit. The Red Sox had won 93 games in 2002, but they missed the playoffs. They wanted to upgrade their hitting to supplement Manny Ramírez and Nomar Garciaparra. On the day they signed me, for one year and $1.25 million, Epstein told a *Boston Globe* reporter, "We think, all the scouts think, he has a very high ceiling. You're looking at a player with the potential to be a middle-of-the-lineup bat in the big leagues." It was nice of him to say, but I wasn't promised a thing. Between me, Kevin Millar, Bill Mueller, Todd Walker — a teammate of mine in Minnesota — and Jeremy Giambi, Epstein had spent just over $10 million for five new players. Plus, Shea Hillenbrand was already in place with the ability to play first and third. The competition for first base, designated hitter, and third base was going to be intense in spring training.

At least I knew exactly where to go in the spring. The Twins trained in Fort Myers and, as luck would have it, so did the Red Sox. So all I had to do was travel across town when it was time to get ready for the 2003 season. But that was the only similarity between the Twins and the Red Sox. As soon as I looked around the Boston clubhouse, I knew I had to become a different player. Everywhere I looked I saw someone working his ass off trying to improve — Manny and Nomar, Jason Varitek, even crazy Derek Lowe. Everyone was working on something, trying to get better.

If the Twins hadn't released me, I wouldn't have had the opportunity to see how a team like that functions. I wouldn't have known that there was something much better out there for me. You never miss what you never had, right? It was eye-opening for me. I was looking at a guy like Manny, already one of the best right-handed hitters ever, already an All-Star, and he was busting his tail. I said to myself, *David Ortiz, you had better get your act together and get to work.* I had been blind to that part of the game, the work that goes into it before and after the game. I talked to myself a lot that spring, just saying, all the time, *I get it now.*

The Red Sox had a new manager for the 2003 season, and his name was Grady Little. He was pulling for me to make it, and I could sense his support. I started off strong in the spring, and when I started to tail off a bit, he sat me down for a private talk.

"What's going on with you?" he asked. "Are you tired or something? You don't look the same."

It was a great observation on his part. I was tired, and I explained the reason to him in one word.

Manny.

I told myself that I wanted to be a great player, and I saw that Manny was already there. I wanted to do what he was doing. I knew that he wasn't really the person he wanted people to think he was. Manny wanted people to think that he was a lazy bastard, because he didn't want anyone to know just how hard he was working. He liked that people described him as kind of an airhead who was great in baseball just because he was a natural at hitting.

One day he said to me, "Come and do my workout with me."

You won't believe the schedule he put me through. At the end of each day, I was pretty much dead. It was nuts. He had a trainer who would get us started around 6:30 or 7:00 each morning. Then we'd play the game. Let's say we'd leave the park around 4:00. We'd go home for an hour or 90 minutes and then meet up with the trainer for *another* two-hour workout.

Man, Manny wore me out. I did that workout for about two and a half weeks and actually started to get used to it. But when I told Grady about it, he asked me to stop. He said he wanted me on his team and he didn't want to give anyone any excuses for not having me in the mix. I certainly understood what he meant. It had been a .137 spring batting average for Minnesota, four years earlier, that convinced them I wasn't ready to be a big leaguer.

But what I was learning from Manny, Pedro, Grady, and eventually Theo Epstein was clear: I was a long way from Minnesota. It was different in spring training, and when I got back to Boston, the intensity of the fans and the ballpark was unlike anything I'd ever experienced from a home crowd. The fans knew all of the players, whether they saw the players at the park or at the grocery store. They were desperate for a championship, and they seemed to be on top of every pitch, every swing, every movement on the field.

I was on a new team, in a new city, and now, for the first time in my career, it was time to see if I could reach in the majors what had come so easily in the minors: greatness.

4

Work, Wait, Play

The best right-handed hitter I've ever seen in my life is Manny Ramírez. I could sit here all day and give you dozens of reasons why, but let's start with the obvious one: in the spring and summer of 2003, he helped me change the way I thought about and played baseball.

I've had many batting coaches in my career, but Manny was the best one I ever had. If you were in a mini-slump, he always understood what the problem was. I'd always known that he was a hitting genius, long before I got to the Red Sox. He was one of the rare power hitters who could do everything. He could hurt you with a line drive over the second baseman's head, an opposite-field home run, or a shot to the power alleys. He put up some absolutely crazy numbers before we became teammates, and after spending some up-close time with him, I could see why.

One year, playing in Cleveland, he drove in 165 runs in 147 games. That's ridiculous. That same season he had 44 home runs and a .333 batting average. All of that and he only finished third in the Most Valuable Player Award voting. The year before I got to the Red Sox, Manny won the batting title with a .349 average, led the league with a .450 on-base percentage, and had a slugging percentage of .647.

Again, ridiculous. And even worse than before, he finished *ninth* in the MVP voting.

What I quickly learned about Manny was that he wasn't going to win many media popularity contests. He loved the way they talked about him, as if he were some airhead who just happened to know how to handle a bat. In fact, he was a thinker in the games, as well as in training sessions and batting practice. He would train for where he knew pitchers liked to go. He almost never pulled the ball in practice because he knew he was unlikely to get that pitch in the games. If he did get it, he already knew what to do with it. The truth is, I would say that 70 percent of today's pitchers don't feel comfortable pitching inside. When pitchers go in now, it's only because they think that you have zero chance of hitting that inside pitch. That's the only intentional reason. The other reason is they make a mistake: they try to go away and the ball comes back in. Watch baseball. Watch the game. Sit down and watch the game and take notes and see how many times you see pitchers pitching inside. They just don't. And with a guy like Manny? They didn't even think about it.

I learned to see the game a different way, just from watching and listening to Manny. He was really good at slowing a pitcher down and knowing what the guy wanted to do. When he was really locked in, he was seeing it in slow motion. Really, it didn't matter what they threw him, or if a righty or lefty was on the mound. He was crushing everybody. I had heard of hitters getting to that level, but I had never experienced it. It was going to be a little while before I got the chance.

I had a lot of time to study his on-field techniques early in 2003 because I wasn't playing. The Red Sox had many players who profiled as first basemen, third basemen, or designated hitters, and I was one of them. Without any promise of playing time. The third basemen were Shea Hillenbrand, who had made the All-Star team the year before, and Bill Mueller, who was hitting over .380 in the first two months of the season. Hillenbrand could also play first, which made room for Mueller but created a jam in the first/DH lane that included me, Kevin Millar, and Jeremy Giambi. It was a bit of a mess. I couldn't figure out what my role was in April and May. I was on pace for just over 300 at-bats, a part-time schedule. It was the only link between my time with the Red Sox and my time with the Twins.

My situation aside, I loved the excitement of Boston. Fenway Park was either full or close to it every time we played, and there was always a Sox fan who knew your name when you were on the road. The fans were smart and intense. None of them were old enough to recall when the team last won the World Series, in 1918, and they hungered for a season to finally end with a win and a parade. Winning the Series was the mission of the city, the whole region really, and there wasn't a week that went by without a reference to it.

There were no places to hide out if you were a big leaguer in New England. Everyone in the region seemed to love baseball and have a strong opinion about it. Every aspect of baseball was discussed in Boston, from the money spent by the owners to the moves of the general manager to the decisions the manager made during the games. No one was above criticism. That was especially true if there was a thought that any well-paid players weren't giving everything they had on the field. There was something about the desperation of the people in Boston that made me want to perform for them. I had never seen fans feeling such an urgent need to win.

The problem at that time was that I saw them more than they saw me. And when they did see me, I wasn't circling the bases. On May 26, Memorial Day, my season home run total stood at two. Grady Little had told me in March to stop doing Manny's workout because I wasn't used to it and it was making me look slower in the games. But now that I wasn't playing, I figured I should at least try to keep up with Manny. And whenever I would get frustrated or didn't feel like putting the work in, Manny and Pedro would be in my ear. "Keep working," they'd say. "You're going to get a chance soon."

I admired Manny and Pedro, but it was hard to watch what was happening. In those first two months, there was no rhythm to my schedule. Sometimes I would start back-to-back games. Sometimes I would pinch-hit. There were days I would play first and days I'd be the DH. Unfortunately, there were too many times when the days would pass — a couple of times it was four days — without me leaving the bench. I liked the city, I liked my manager, and I liked my team-mates. I hated watching.

One day in late May, I called my agent and left him a blunt message: "If you're not here, in Boston, by tomorrow, you're fired!" To his credit, he arrived for breakfast the next day. I had already told Grady that I was better than the players who were on the field in front of me. He knew how angry I was. So I wanted my agent to set up a meeting with Theo Epstein. I told Theo how I was feeling and that something needed to happen, and maybe that meant trading or releasing me.

There was nothing calm about my demeanor. I knew that I could play, that I could really hit, and I wanted my chance. I knew I was ready. I wasn't always in the best shape in Minnesota, and now I was. I didn't have the mental approach in Minnesota that I was gaining in Boston, and I wanted to put that to work on the field. Things were starting to click for me, in the way I thought about and approached the game. I was 27 and should have been ready for my prime. If I could hit 20 home runs in Minnesota without even getting 500 at-bats, I felt that I should be capable of more in Boston playing all the time.

I didn't back down from Theo. I wanted to play. I wanted to know what he was going to do about it. Theo was my age, in his first full season as general manager. He was young and inexperienced, but he handled the confrontation like a veteran. He told me that he believed in my ability, that he always had as far back as the late 1990s, when he was working in San Diego and I was in the minors. He told me he needed some time to make some moves and then I would get my opportunity.

He was a man of his word. On May 29, Hillenbrand was traded to Arizona. Hillenbrand had actually been playing well between first and third, and he had driven in the most runs on our team. But Hillenbrand's less-patient approach didn't fit into what we were building as far as our identity as a team, and although a lot of people tried to label it "new school" baseball, it really was what Manny had been doing all along. Slow pitchers down. Be patient and see as many pitches as possible. Find a way to smash your pitch or, at worst, get on base. Our whole team was good at that — so good that it became the best offense I'd ever seen.

When Hillenbrand was traded, for pitcher Byun-Hyun Kim, Mueller became the everyday third baseman. Millar got the bulk of the at-bats at first. And for the first time in my career, I felt that, from top to bottom, a team was saying to me, "The job is yours. Go get it, big boy." I pinch-hit occasionally and I played some first, but I was officially the full-time designated hitter of the Red Sox. I took a lot of pride in preparing for the job.

Now the only time I sat down was when the team was in the field. I spent a lot of time analyzing pitchers, and I never had to do it by myself. Pedro was our best pitcher, and one of the smartest people in baseball. I used to tell people that he had a mind from NASA. That's the best way to describe him. He's such a talented, intelligent person. When he wasn't pitching, he'd often come up to me and say, "Start looking for the slider or the cutter. He's going to throw it to you your next at-bat." I'd ask him how he knew that and he'd say, "Because of what he did to you your last at-bat."

So I'd go up for my next at-bat, wait on the pitch that Pedro told me to wait on, and hit a home run. The crowd would go crazy, and I'd run the bases, all the while thinking, *How in the hell does Pedro know this stuff?*

I was so grateful to be able to learn valuable lessons about the game from Pedro and Manny, in person. Not only did God give Pedro a gift to play baseball, He also gave him a lot of guts. I was able to get a good idea of what Boston fans look for by watching Pedro. He was a great pitcher, and he played like he was trying to prove something. But who knows who Pedro would have been if the Dodgers had not traded him? I tell him that the Dodgers did him a favor when they gave up on a Hall of Fame pitcher. They provided him with an extra edge, and maybe that would never have happened if he had stayed in L.A.

Between getting tips from Pedro and Manny and getting actual playing time every day, the game had started to slow down for me. I was so obsessed with learning, figuring out the tendencies, knowing what a pitcher wanted to do against me. It seriously got to the point where I would be dreaming about hitting. It was all I thought about. That was dangerous, but in a good way. My confidence was rising to levels I had only heard people describe but didn't think I'd ever experience. Every mistake that was thrown to me, I felt, was going to be a home run. It was as if everyone else was trying to move fast but I was seeing the ball in slow motion. You ever see that special effect in the movies? Everything slows down and you can do whatever you want. That's exactly how it started to be. I would be like, *Yeah, throw me that changeup. Here comes the changeup. POW.* Or, *Oh, you throw ninety-eight? Throw me that fastball. Here comes the fastball. POW.* It was like that.

Besides the preparation and playing time, there were many other reasons I found that groove. Our lineup was impossible to face at times. One through nine, we had guys who made pitching staffs uncomfortable: Johnny Damon, Todd Walker, Nomar Garciaparra,

Manny, me, Trot Nixon, Millar, Jason Varitek, and Bill Mueller. Half-way through the year, reporters began to notice that we were slugging so well that we were exceeding the pace of one of the most famous teams in history, the 1927 New York Yankees. That team had an intimidating nickname, Murderers' Row, and featured Lou Gehrig and Babe Ruth in the lineup. They finished with a .489 team slugging percentage; ours was .491.

And that brings me back to Manny. If he was anywhere close to me in the lineup, the job got that much easier. If Manny was hitting behind you, the pitcher would give you something to hit because he didn't want to put you on base and then have to deal with Manny. If Manny was hitting in front of you, he got on base so much that there were always opportunities to drive in runs. That's what happened for me as the spring turned into summer.

On the first day of summer, June 21, my home run total for the season still wasn't great. I had only three, and my slugging percentage was .480. Two months later, I was at 18 home runs with a .545 slugging percentage. I was just getting warmed up. I finished the season with 31 home runs, the highest number of my career. I finished fifth in the MVP voting, one slot ahead of Manny.

It was more than the individual success, though. We had a good team, and we believed we could win the World Series. Our fans also believed in us. It was all so new, both to them and to many of us. We were unlike any other Red Sox team in recent memory. We were relatable and playful, aware of the long rivalry with the Yankees but not overwhelmed by it. During the regular season, in fact, I had some of my best games against the Yankees. We weren't afraid of them.

Sometimes I thought back to my time in Minnesota and wondered what could have been if I'd stayed there. As I started to get hot with the Red Sox, one of the reporters from the Twin Cities came to Boston for a story. I remember he asked, "Why are you having success here and you didn't have it in Minnesota?" I don't know if I answered this way, but I wanted to say, "Did you just look at the games or did you actually watch them?"

If you look at my last year in Minnesota, I was going in this direction. I was hurt and I didn't play all the time, yet I had 20 home runs in fewer than 500 at-bats. Give me a chance to play and I'm going to produce.

Boston was the right combination of everything. Fenway is the smallest park in the majors, but I looked up at the end of June and we had already drawn 1.3 million fans. They couldn't get enough of us. Grady wasn't a micromanager from the dugout. He showed confidence in his players and wasn't afraid to walk around the clubhouse telling jokes. Our pitching was good, led by Pedro and his league-leading earned run average, but if you can believe it, our offense was better. Besides the record slugging percentage, we averaged about six runs per game. Even teams with superstar pitching staffs knew it was going to be hard to silence us over the course of a series. It was a fun group. We didn't win the American League East, but we got a playoff spot via the wild card.

We began the playoffs with a five-game series against the Oakland A's. They were a good team, and one day their bench coach, Terry Francona, would be one of us. But that wasn't the focus going into October. We felt that we matched up well against any team, and we thought we were going to see the Yankees in the next round. I was all right with all of it.

I was 27 years old, playing every day, and in my prime. I had found my game in Boston. And finally, for the first time since I had left the DR, I felt like I had found a home.

5

Turning Point

I couldn't do anything, which isn't like me. Anyone who has ever been around me understands how much appreciation I have for well-timed jokes, continuous laughter, good music, and being social with smiling friends. I can't think of a better place than New York City to do all those things, and more, at all hours of the day. But there I was the night of October 15, 2003, in the middle of Manhattan, with an appetite for . . . nothing.

I couldn't relax.

I couldn't go to one of my favorite Dominican restaurants, Café Rubio in Queens, and eat rice and beans, chased with some red wine.

No music, no matter how riveting and rhythmic the bass line, was right for the moment.

I turned to TV and wasn't comforted by familiar shows and old movies.

There wasn't anywhere in all of New York City I wanted to go. There are more Dominicans in the city, close to 675,000, than there are people in Boston, and the community has always been good to me. Most of my friends there are Yankees fans, and yet I'd often see them in the crowd, with their Yankees hats on, cheering for me after a home run. I always had a good time with them afterward, teasing them about being confused and their ability to root for both the Red Sox and Yankees, which is supposed to be impossible.

It was the night before Game 7 of the American League Championship Series at Yankee Stadium, and I was in my Westin Times Square hotel room, with the possibilities of the next day spinning in my head.

"Aren't we going out?" a few of my boys asked.

"Nah," I told them. "I'm going to stay right here."

I couldn't get the game out of my head. Our regular-season match-ups with the Yankees were already intense enough, but these six games we'd played in the series were more intense than ever. I'd never seen anything like it. This was two teams who respected each other, literally fighting for the pennant and a chance to win the World Series. We had thrown at them and they had thrown at us. Their 72-year-old bench coach, Don Zimmer, had run out of the dugout and chased after our ace, Pedro Martínez, because he thought Pedro was trying to intimidate the Yankees by being a headhunter. Manny Ramírez had pointed and yelled at Roger Clemens because he thought Clemens was trying to hit him with an inside pitch. Two of their players, Karim García and Jeff Nelson, even got into a fight with a part-time groundskeeper at Fenway.

Why did these things happen? Because it was Boston versus New York, and when those two cities are mentioned side by side, it's never a neutral conversation. After spending the spring, summer, and fall in Boston, I had finally begun to grasp what I had gotten myself into. When I was in Minneapolis, Tiffany and I used to go across the street from the Metrodome to a bar called Buff's Pub. We'd go there to eat chicken wings, have beers, and watch TV. Buff's also provided free self-serve popcorn. One time I remember going back to the popcorn machine to serve myself seconds and a customer came up to me and requested another serving. He thought I worked there. Keep in mind that I was in the same neighborhood where the Twins play half of

their games. I was never recognized there, though, and it wasn't because I was trying to keep a low profile. That just wasn't the culture
of baseball fans there. If it was, I didn't experience it. So, officially,
as a member of the Twins, my popcorn requests outnumbered my
autograph requests when I was at Buff's.

Contrast that with Boston. The three of us — Tiffany, our daughter
Alex, who was two years old at the time, and me — were living in a
tiny Garrison Square apartment. I thought if they didn't know me
after six years in the Twin Cities, why would anyone in Boston know
me after six weeks? But when Tiffany and Alex ran errands, people
would see Tiffany's last name and make the connection with the new
Red Sox player. They just knew. They even knew what I might be able
to bring to the team.

As I sat in my hotel room, I thought of how far I'd come since
that angry meeting with Theo Epstein five months earlier. I was convinced that he'd endorsed playing Jeremy Giambi over me because of
the novelty of a Giambi playing for both the Red Sox and Yankees. I
swear I thought that was the reason. If we'd been the team with Jason
Giambi, I might have been able to understand. But playing behind
Jeremy Giambi was a circus, and the only reason I could find for the
Red Sox to play him over me was his last name. Was it true? I wasn't
willing to shrug it off and say that it wasn't.

You have to understand how much time I'd spent venting to the
people closest to me. Tiffany spent several nights simply listening as I
ranted about being a backup to players I knew I was better than. Most
baseball wives and girlfriends can relate to what Tiffany was experiencing. This is a hard game with a lot of public commentary attached
to it. Our spouses see and hear us without any filter. They hear about
frustrations and politics that a lot of fans never consider. When I was
in the minors, Tiffany used to sift through the newspapers looking
for negative articles about me. If she found any, she would try to hide
them. Knowing what she was up to, I'd ask her to cut them out and

put them up on the refrigerator. I often used doubt as motivation, whether I was in Salt Lake City or Boston. Tiffany was always supportive, and she never discouraged me from taking my case to Grady Little, Epstein, or even ownership if necessary.

Fortunately, I had Pedro and Manny on my side. Pedro was incredible. When I talk to Tiffany now about the 2003 season, she says, "Thank you, Pedro Martínez." She says that because she knows that he used his leverage to get me on the field. After one of his starts, against Philadelphia in June, when he pitched well and our unpredictable bullpen blew his lead on the way to a loss, he pulled me aside and told me he was taking me to dinner. He could see that I was angry about my uncertain status, and he wanted to cheer me up. We saw the end of the game in the clubhouse and then showered and dressed before the media entered to ask their questions about what had just happened. Pedro had decided, weeks earlier, not to speak regularly with reporters, and after that tough loss, I think there was media resentment that the starting pitcher wasn't there to give his perspective on the game. There was resentment from some veterans on the team too. A rumor had started that we left the park before the game ended, which wasn't true, and so some of the veterans viewed our absence as a lack of support for teammates who had lost a game and now had to answer for it without the starting pitcher. They took their complaints to the manager's office.

Once again, you have to weigh the politics of a baseball clubhouse. The veterans were mostly upset with Pedro, but he was the ace and just a handful of players were willing to criticize him. I was an easier target. I was new. My baseball résumé was light. And I was a part-timer. Pedro rushed into Little's office when he found out that I had been scratched from the lineup as some type of punishment for leaving the ballpark while the game was still going on (which I hadn't actually done).

"If he doesn't play when I'm pitching," Pedro told the manager, "then I'm going to refuse to pitch. I want him out there. He's a good hitter, and I want to win."

They didn't have to listen to me. But Pedro? His opinions meant something, and if he wanted me to play when he pitched, that was the way it was going to be.

When he wasn't doing things like that at the park, he was treating Tiffany and me like family members when we were at his home. He lived in a Chestnut Hill mansion then, and whenever there was a weekend or early afternoon game, he'd invite us over to eat, listen to music, and watch movies. He knew our tastes, so there would be beans and rice for Tiffany and his sister would make goat for me. Sometimes the place was like a bustling day care center: our daughter, Pedro's kids, his nieces and nephews, and Manny's children would all be running around the huge basement at Pedro's place. As much as getting on the field in Boston had been a struggle, I knew in New England that I had what felt like genuine relatives with Pedro, Manny, and their families.

As the season progressed, both my playing time and my Boston education increased. I already mentioned that Pedro rarely talked with the media, and Manny didn't either. Nomar Garciaparra was uncomfortable with the media attention, and he had been friendly with Ted Williams, another Red Sox superstar who had a strained relationship with most reporters. I'd heard stories about Carl Yastrzemski and Jim Rice and Roger Clemens, all Boston stars who had decided that they'd had enough of the people who were paid to write and talk about baseball. I wasn't knowledgeable enough about the Boston media to identify the core of the problem. What was it about playing in Boston that made players so skeptical about what was being reported? I didn't get it, and I was several years away from getting it. At the time I thought it was something I'd never have to worry about because I can get along with a variety of personality types. Also, I wasn't perceived as the team spokesman then. When you're one of the superstars, the expectation is that you'll be there to answer for everything, even things that don't directly involve you.

None of that was on my mind as I sat in my hotel room. I wasn't a star, but I was bearing a star's burden that night. All I could think about was my game plan against Clemens, New York's Game 7 starter. We had Pedro going for us, so I wasn't worried about our pitching. What were we going to do, and what was I going to do in the final game of the series?

On the day of the game I felt the pressure of the moment, but I wasn't nervous. There's a big difference between nerves and pressure. I liked the pressure. I liked the stage, especially in New York. It was strange to a lot of people, but my teammates could see how excited I would get if there was a situation in a game where we were tied or down by a run and I had a chance to win it. I always want that situation, and I thought Game 7 might provide it.

I'd heard a lot of stories about Clemens and the legendary things he had accomplished in a dozen years playing for the Red Sox. He was 40 years old in 2003, and still one of the best pitchers in baseball. Our team matched up well against him, so I knew we'd be able to put together some good at-bats and get him out of the game early. That's exactly what happened in the top of the fourth inning. Trot Nixon hit a home run off him in the second, and Kevin Millar homered in the fourth. We were ahead 4–0, and Clemens was done for the night. That was the good news. I'll tell you what wasn't good, though, at least not for me: seeing the next pitcher.

It was Mike Mussina. In the first 20 at-bats of my career against Mussina, I didn't get a hit. The more I faced him the more comfortable I started to get, but he's one of the toughest pitchers I have ever faced. He threw 95 miles per hour, had great stuff, and had excellent location. I think he's a Hall of Famer, for sure, and he pitched like it in Game 7. He gave the Yankees three innings of relief work and didn't give up a run. He kept his team close when it felt like we had a chance to pile up a bunch of runs and make it an easy win.

Pedro was pitching the way that I knew he would. Not only is he one of the most talented athletes to ever play baseball, he's highly intelligent as well. He was a psychologist on the mound. He knew, based on their patterns, what hitters wanted to do, and so he would never give them a pitching pattern. He could master four pitches, at any time, so you never knew what to expect. I used to tell him that his brain was scary. On his off days, he was a student. He'd sit in the dugout watching to see what the opposing starter's sequence was. If I sat next to him after my first at-bat, he could already tell me what was going to happen the rest of the game. For example, if a pitcher threw a great breaking ball for a strike and then didn't throw it again, Pedro would identify that pitch as the weapon that the pitcher wanted to use in the next key situation. "The way he approached you in the first inning," he'd say, "was only to get you later on. He's trying to get you to chase so he doesn't have to use his real good one until he needs it." In the meantime, that pitcher would try to nibble, or make a batter get himself out. If he couldn't do that and you got him to, say, a hitter's count with a runner on base, the Pedro Theory was to look for the secret weapon on the next pitch. I hit many home runs due to the intelligence of Pedro.

In Game 7, Pedro had pitched seven innings and allowed just two runs, a pair of Jason Giambi solo homers. As he left the mound at the end of the seventh, with a 4–2 lead, he pointed to the heavens and thanked God. We were six outs away from bringing the American League pennant to Boston for the first time in 18 years.

The story got better in the top of the eighth. Mussina was out of the game, and the Yankees were on to their fifth pitcher of the night, David Wells. I knew what New York manager Joe Torre was trying to do. He started the eighth with reliever Jeff Nelson, a right-hander, to face Manny. Once Nelson got Manny to ground out, Torre called for Wells, a lefty, to get me. But I didn't have a problem picking up the ball against any of the Yankee lefties, so I swung at the first pitch I saw from Wells. It soared over the right-field wall for a home run and a 5–2 lead.

I didn't realize it at the time, but what happened next would change my entire career. What happened next led to some revelations about the city in which I played and the kind of player I was going to become in that city. No question, we thought we were going to win the game. Pedro thought he had finished pitching for the night, but Grady Little asked him to go back out for the bottom of the eighth. That's where the problems began. Pedro was able to get an out, but he gave up a double to Derek Jeter after getting two quick strikes on him. That wasn't Pedro's style, even against a great hitter like Jeter. If Pedro had you in a hole, his combination of brains and talent was usually too much for a hitter to overcome. The hit was a sign that Pedro was getting tired.

When Bernie Williams singled to drive in Jeter and make the score 5–3, the stadium erupted to life. The crowd knew that this was the best chance the Yankees were going to have in what was left of the game, and so the stadium was as loud at that moment as I'd ever heard it. At that moment, Grady made his only mistake of the night, but it was a big one: he asked Pedro if he could stay in the game.

You can't ask an athlete that question. That's like asking a hitter who is 0-for-20 against a pitcher, "Hey, do you want me to pinch-hit for you here?" What are you supposed to say? You always think you have a chance, and you're not going to back down from a challenge. The only thing to do is take it out of the athlete's hands and make the decision for him.

Pedro stayed in the game. Even though he was still throwing hard, the at-bats from the Yankees became tougher. By the time the eighth inning was over, Pedro was out of the game and a 5–2 lead for us had become a 5–5 tie. I couldn't believe it, after we had controlled most of the game. It reached its worst point in the bottom of the 11th inning, when Aaron Boone ended our season with a home run to left field off Tim Wakefield.

I was sick. Too sick to be angry. Too sick to be analytical. Too sick to immediately replay, step by step, what had gone wrong in the game. I know a lot of longtime Boston fans thought that the team was cursed, that somehow that was the reason for the loss. I didn't think like that, and neither did any of my teammates. We knew that there was nothing mysterious about beating the Yankees and that we had been in position to do it. Until that eighth inning.

When that home run in the 11th started to rise toward left field, it felt like it hung there forever. I kept hoping that a sudden wind would knock it down, or that it would take a hard left turn and go foul.

I was drained, and so was our team. Our normal clubhouse had a loud, unrestrained spirit to it. On that night, we were the quietest club in all of New York City. We slowly faced the finality of our season. We were not preparing to play the Florida Marlins in the World Series. We were just going home.

I still didn't get it then. I had no idea that the New England fans were as hungry as they were, that they felt the pain of the loss just like we did. I had never seen so much passion from fans in my career. When I got back to Boston, I could see how crushed everyone was. My neighbors, postal workers, people at the grocery store, newscasters. I saw the sadness on all of those faces, and that's when I finally understood what Boston was about and who I was playing for. I was devastated, and so were they. I knew then that I was going to work harder than I ever had in my career. We had to win, for us and for them. I never wanted to see faces that sad again.

6

The New Red Sox

My wife knows more than anyone just how restless my off-season nights used to be.

Sometimes she would find me awake and thinking about future at-bats when I should have been asleep. There in the dark, I'd think about all the pitchers I was likely to face the next season and in the playoffs. I didn't just want to know every pitch they threw; I wanted to anticipate the exact moments when they would want to throw them. I wanted all the information I could get. The separation between us and the Yankees was slim, so slim that winning the pennant might come down to the recognition of a single pitch.

To learn those kinds of details, I would need to do extra video work. And then there would also have to be a disciplined running, stretching, and lifting program. I couldn't wait until spring training, or even Thanksgiving, to accomplish all of that. Everywhere I went, I could feel and hear the frustrations of Red Sox fans. What I loved about them was that they wanted the same thing I did—greatness and a championship. They talked about it all the time, and I thought about it all the time, so we were the perfect match. I was willing to sacrifice sleep and a relaxing vacation to get there.

It didn't matter that our season had been over for two weeks. I still couldn't stop myself from considering all the things I needed to do to help us be at least one game, or one pitch, better than the Yankees. Tiffany would tell people that I worked harder than anyone she'd ever met, but she still wanted me to slow down.

"What are you doing awake?" she would sleepily ask. My reply was always the same: "I'm getting ahead of the game." In reality, I don't think I ever felt like I got ahead at all. I just didn't want to be playing catchup in February.

I never imagined that in late October 2003 someone would already be ahead of me. I never imagined that my own team would be far more anxious and active than I was. The Game 7 loss to the Yankees had torn me up, knowing that we were just five outs away from going to the World Series. Anytime I got close to contentment, I'd feel the sting of that loss. I'd remember the extended roar of Yankee Stadium after they tied the score at 5 in the eighth, how the park seemed to shake when they won it in the 11th with that Aaron Boone home run, and how quiet that short plane ride back to Boston had been. Those memories always pushed me to work overtime.

The Red Sox had already begun making their moves with two quick ones that led to what was about to become a parade of transactions. One of them, I thought, was a mistake. The other one was simply a power move to get a player's attention.

A week and a half after the letdown in New York, the Red Sox decided against bringing back Grady Little as manager. I thought they were crazy. He made one mistake, and it was like ownership took it personally. That shows how much I know.

I thought he should have gotten a contract extension. Everyone could see that Grady stayed with Pedro Martínez too long against the Yankees, but I think more people should have pointed out that he was putting his faith in the best pitcher in baseball. Our bullpen had been great in the postseason, but what would have been said if Grady had taken out Pedro and the bullpen had given it up? *Why'd you take Pedro out and put that guy in?* Grady was a great communicator, and he didn't always make his decisions based on statistics or matchups. The principal team owners, John Henry, Tom Werner, and Larry Lucchino, didn't like that about him. Neither did Theo Epstein, the general manager. I learned during the season that there were also things that Grady didn't like about them. They were often stat-driven when it came to the game, while he relied on his experience in clubhouses and dugouts. His focus was on relationships. He wanted to run the team his way, and he thought Theo and ownership liked to meddle.

I remember one time he called me into his office early in 2003, when I wasn't a starter, and briefly explained what it was like for him to manage the Red Sox. "You do understand that you'd be playing every day if it were up to me, right?" he told me. "I don't make out the lineup. I wish I did. It comes from upstairs. But I want you to keep working because I feel that your chance is coming. I'm fighting for you."

If I needed reminders of the differences between big- and small-market teams, Grady's exit was one of them. It was hard for me to grasp. I felt the anger toward him in Boston as soon as we returned from New York. You couldn't turn on the radio — sports radio or news radio — without hearing someone vent about Grady and how he'd ruined the season. Clearly, most Red Sox fans put the Game 7 loss on him. But I saw a manager who always believed in me, who guided a team to the playoffs for the first time in four seasons, and who encouraged bringing fun and unity to a clubhouse that had become joyless and divided over the years. And I kept coming back to this: who fires a manager who's one game away from the World Series? If I'm a managerial candidate and I see that a guy gets fired after being one game away from the Series, my first thought should be, *Fuck, no thank you.* Seriously. You're telling me that if I don't make the playoffs I'm out? Even if I'm managing in the American League

East, one of the toughest and richest divisions in baseball? In big markets, patience is for someone else. Get the job done quickly and consistently, or else you're expendable. That goes for managers and players both.

Manny Ramírez, who I thought of as an idol, found that out a few days after Grady left. I had a hard time taking the news seriously, but it was true: the Red Sox had placed Manny on waivers. That meant that any team in baseball could claim Manny as their own, as long as it was willing to pay the remainder of his contract, which was about $95 million.

Manny had his quirks, and anyone who spent any time in our clubhouse knew about them. He was my boy, and yet he still did things to me that most people would have called rude. But it was Manny. You always forgave him. For example, I can't tell you how many times he would say to me, "Papi, let's meet for lunch." It would be his idea, and he'd even suggest the time and place. I'd arrive and wait for 20 minutes, 40 minutes, sometimes even an hour. No Manny. I'd call him and he'd say, "Hey, Papi! I'm at the park." As if we never had plans. That was Manny, though, talented, lovable, and unpredictable.

He wasn't just a special hitter who was fun to watch. There was also something about his aura that caused fans to fall in love with him from afar. I can't think of any other player who could get away with some of the adventures he had in the outfield; instead of booing, people would clap and laugh. But the Red Sox were tired of the unpredictable side of him, and after they got word that Manny said he wanted to play for the Yankees, they put him on waivers, knowing that neither the Yankees nor anyone else would take on his big contract.

All of us in the Red Sox organization were similarly obsessed with the Yankees. We all had different ways of dealing with it. It was hard to avoid thinking or talking about them, and not only because of the last game of our 2003 season. This was a team that played in our division, had appeared in six of the previous eight World Series, and had won four of them. I respected them, and I loved playing against them. They brought out a side of me that I didn't know I had until I got to Boston. I've always been someone who loves winning and expects to win, but I became a bull when I got to the Red Sox. It was this animal instinct, this daily background mentality, that I wanted to beat teams' asses. All the energy I had was devoted to becoming a champion.

Management was committed to tinkering with the team, reshaping it, and spending what seemed like endless streams of cash. Shortly after Manny went unclaimed, there were rumors that the Red Sox still wanted to move on from him and were trying to trade him. And not just him, but Nomar Garciaparra, who was one of the most popular players in New England. They had already signed Oakland closer Keith Foulke and traded for Arizona starter Curt Schilling. They had also hired a new manager, Terry Francona, whom I'd never met. He had a reputation for being friendly and smart, someone who could nicely blend the statistical interests of the front office and the day-to-day rhythm of the clubhouse. His father had played in the big leagues for 14 years, so Tito had been around the game since he was a little boy. His father had played with Joe Torre, and a preteen Tito had been in the clubhouse with both of them. Now, nearly 40 years later, Tito would be part of the biggest rivalry in baseball and managing against New York and Torre.

Tito was going to have a good team to manage. We all knew that. What we didn't know was who his shortstop and left fielder would be. For a month and a half, the Red Sox tried to trade for Alex Rodriguez, who was a great shortstop with the Rangers. Honestly, it blew my mind. Things were happening so fast that I couldn't keep up with what the Red Sox were thinking. First, I thought the whole A-Rod-to-Boston idea was unrealistic. When I found out it was real, I convinced myself that we were just going to add him to the lineup we already had and maybe put him at third. Finally, I had to accept the reality of what they wanted to do: A-Rod and Magglio Ordóñez coming in and Nomar, Manny, and pitching prospect Jon Lester going out.

I didn't like any of that.

To understand why, ownership and the front office needed to be on the field to see the looks when pitchers knew they had to get through Manny and me in the lineup. They knew we were a dangerous duo, the heart of an already great lineup. There was no way around it: most pitchers were afraid of us. What bothered me was the idea that you could just swap out successful players in Boston and still expect to be close to winning the World Series. It doesn't work that way. Why would you willingly take away the heart of a lineup?

Frankly, Boston can be a negative atmosphere at times, and you've got to be mentally strong enough to handle it. I've seen players, really good players, come through Boston and it changed them. Some of them were scared of the intensity and high expectations. Some of them were too sensitive. Some of them wanted out.

Would A-Rod have been different? Maybe. I'm glad I didn't have to find out. The negotiations to bring A-Rod to Boston broke down, so Manny, Nomar, and Lester stayed in place and A-Rod went to . . . the Yankees. The rivalry didn't need anything else added to it, and now it had an easy reality TV story line of a great player flirting with one team and eventually landing with its number-one enemy.

We didn't worry about any of that as we prepared for the 2004 season. We loved our team. I mean that in the truest sense of the word. I think one of the things that transformed our clubhouse was the deep love and respect we had for one another.

One of the small but important changes we brought to the team was going out of our way to celebrate one another. I'd heard many stories about how some Red Sox teams had been a collection of good guys who were more comfortable being individuals than giving themselves to the team. We weren't going to let that happen to us. It started in 2003, and it was going to continue in 2004. When Manny hit a home run, we weren't just going to high-five him; we were going to hug him. We hugged when Pedro finished a strong outing. We hugged after a great defensive play by Johnny Damon. Really, hugging is my nature. I'd noticed that in America, for some people, hugging was common only when something bad happened. That didn't make sense to me. With all the time players spend at the ballpark, we are each other's second family. Let's have fun, win, not be so dry about our celebrations, and show how much we care about one another. I know that as a fan, when I see guys expressing themselves like that in the dugout, it makes me happy.

We also knew that this was going to be the last year with this group in place. Our team was filled with players in the final year of their contract, and we knew not everyone was going to sign with the Red Sox. Pedro, Nomar, Derek Lowe, and Jason Varitek were among the players in the final season of their contract.

I wasn't in that category because in May 2004 I signed a two-year deal with a team option for a third. Tiffany and I took a while to process what the contract meant. It wasn't just the money, which was a blessing. It was getting a real commitment from a franchise, which we had gotten used to *not* having our first seven years in the big leagues. Even after my breakout 2003 season, we didn't feel like we were settled. But when the contract came, we started thinking for the first time about really settling in. We had moved from Garrison Square in 2003 to the Charles River Apartments in 2004, and Tiffany was excited to purchase what she called our "we made it" items, like a mattress (we had rented one in 2003) and some pots and pans. We could finally think about our first New England home too.

We'd bought a house in Wisconsin, near Tiffany's parents, thinking that we'd make that our base. Now it was time to think about buying something closer to the job.

In some ways, I was settling in more than I knew. And it started with my terrible memory for first names. I saw last names on uniforms all the time, so I could remember all of them easily. But first names? It was crazy. My teammates used to playfully quiz me so they could laugh about what I didn't know. "Tell me my first name right now," they would say. Everyone would laugh when I'd shrug and say I didn't know. To compensate for not knowing names, I'd call everyone "papi." *Hey, papi. How ya doing?* That word, "papi," took over our clubhouse, and it became associated with me.

Thus the birth of Big Papi.

At work, I was starting to understand the personality of the new manager. I was in a bit of a rut at the plate, so one day I took early batting practice. After I took a few swings, I looked behind the cage and saw Tito watching me intently. I took another swing and turned again. He was still locked in, not saying anything, not talking to anyone. After I'd finished, I asked him if he had some advice for me. He was so attentive, he must have seen something.

His response surprised me.

"Who me? Give you advice?" he said. "Did you ever see my numbers in the big leagues? I was terrible! What the hell am I going to tell you? You're one of the greatest, man. Just go out there and keep swinging and have fun."

Then he walked away.

He had no idea how much confidence he gave me with that exchange. His message to me was that he knew I was going to figure it out and that he was going to stay out of the way. He was more interested in making fun of himself than overcomplicating things. I appreciated what he did for me that day. I took off after that, and so did our team.

On July 10, I already had 77 runs batted in, which was tied for the American League lead. Our record was 48-37, and we trailed the Yankees by six games. I was a few days away from playing in my first All-Star Game. More important, on that day, a Saturday, I was in Boston at Beth Israel Hospital for another first: the birth of my third child and only son, D'Angelo. He was a healthy boy, weighing seven pounds and one ounce. In baseball, you never know where you're going to be when that call comes, so I'm grateful that the team was in town so I could be there for such a beautiful moment. When Tiffany said that he was a smaller version of me, she was talking about resemblance. But also like me, it seemed that young D'Angelo never slept, and maybe that was his way of telling us that there were many late nights ahead as we charged toward the playoffs.

One of the events along the way was a mild surprise. As I said, we were playing good baseball, but something was apparently missing from our team. Theo Epstein decided that our overall defense wasn't good enough, so after an off-season of hearing that Nomar might be traded, we finally learned at the end of July that he was being moved. He was off to the Cubs, and his departure signaled just how temporary the label "franchise player" could be. Think about it. Nomar had been in Boston before most people in our organization. He preceded ownership, our general manager, Pedro, Manny, and me. He was beloved by the fans, always hustling and playing hard. He had a loving relationship with Ted Williams, and it was easy to see one of the things they had in common. Man, could Nomar hit. He was a batting champion and perennial MVP candidate. One moment he was going to get a long-term contract from the Red Sox, then you started hearing about trade rumors, and then he was gone.

It was stunning if you looked at it that way, and that's why it can be so hard to relax in professional sports. You never see the changes coming. I knew there wouldn't be any other moves in 2004, but I was close enough to Pedro and Manny to understand that one or both of them could be gone in 2005. I was determined to enjoy the present and help the Red Sox finally win a championship. After the Nomar trade and a series of deals, my new teammates were Orlando Cabrera, Dave Roberts, and Doug Mientkiewicz. Cabrera fit right into our culture with his fun-loving nature and exuberance. He was also one of the best I'd ever seen at hitting behind a runner and moving him over a base. Roberts brought elite base-running ability off the bench. He'd been having a great season with the Dodgers, stealing 33 bases and being caught just once. And Mientkiewicz was part of my family from our days in Minnesota. We practically grew up together with the Twins, and our wives remained close friends even after we left the Twin Cities. I'll admit that I let myself dream some about how meaningful it would be to win a title in Boston with Doug.

With the way we were playing at the end of the season, I didn't think anyone would be able to keep us from a championship. We won 37 of our final 51 games, and I was even better than I had been in 2003. I was at the point where I was visualizing where the ball was going to go before I went to the plate. I didn't just tell myself that I was going to hit the ball to the opposite field. I'd think things like, *I'm going to hit it to the opposite field, and it's going over the fence.* I finished with 41 home runs, 47 doubles, and 139 RBIs. Manny had 43 homers, 44 doubles, and 130 RBIs. Neither A-Rod nor Magglio Ordóñez came close to that kind of production in 2004.

Manny could be a goofball at times, but at least he was on our side. He and Pedro were so talented and thoughtful at their crafts. They had taught me so much about studying pitchers, detecting pitch sequences, and setting a pitcher up in the first at-bat for something you want to do in the third at-bat.

I could feel it as we began our playoff run in Los Angeles against the Angels. We had finished the regular season with 98 wins, three behind the Yankees. But I still thought we were the best team in baseball. We just had to prove it. I trusted all of my teammates, so I knew the postseason stage wasn't too big for any of us. I knew that. What I didn't know was how we were going to perform on that stage, and I didn't even come close to predicting that it would be a performance no one had ever seen before.

7

The October of Ortiz

The first playoff games of October hadn't even been played yet, but everyone, except for the Anaheim Angels and Minnesota Twins, could see where things were headed. It was inevitable. It was going to be the Red Sox and Yankees, again, in the league championship series. The two of us had the most expensive rosters in the game, totaling over $300 million in payroll. We were easily the two highest run producers in baseball. We'd tried to sign and trade for the same players. And we had more ownership and front-office pressure to win than any other two organizations in sports. It made sense that our seasons would be measured by what we'd be able to do against each other.

For us, the Angels were in the way. For the Yankees, it was my old team, the Twins. It's not unusual for a surprise team, an underdog, to get hot in the fall and win the postseason. But 2004 wasn't the year for that. The assembled talent on the Red Sox and Yankees was greater than anything I'd ever seen in baseball. You should never say "no way" in sports, but . . . there was no way either team was going to lose in the division series.

Although the Angels technically had home-field advantage, with the first two games at their place, think about who they were facing.

In Game 1, our starter was Curt Schilling, whose postseason earned run average going into that game was 1.66. Filthy. In Game 2, we had Pedro. A normal Pedro, the best thinker with the best stuff in baseball, is tough enough. But this was Pedro possibly pitching his last season with the Red Sox. He was in the final year of his contract, and it didn't look like the Red Sox were going to come close to meeting the terms he wanted on a new deal. I had spent so much time with him over Sunday evening dinners with our families and on the road with our teammates, so I knew just how driven he was to walk away from Boston being called a winner. We still were going to have our fun, on the field and in the clubhouse. But we also expected to win the World Series.

The first two games went almost perfectly. Schilling gave up just two earned runs in his start, and we backed him up by scoring seven runs in the top of the fourth inning. Pedro gave us seven innings and three runs in his start, and we put the game away with a four-run ninth. We left Anaheim worry-free. We won those games by a combined score of 17–6. When Schilling appeared to tweak his right ankle as he fielded a ground ball, it never occurred to us that the injury would lead to one of the most dramatic stories in the history of the postseason.

Back in Boston, we had the same expectation as the fans. Short series. As usual, Fenway was loud and packed. For the past year and a half, the park had been sold out for each game. I loved playing there, especially when we were in close games late and I had a chance to win it. The park is built in such a way that you feel like you can have conversations with individual fans. Well, there was a guy who always sat behind the plate at Fenway. Always. Every time I walked up for a big at-bat, I'd search for him because I could count on him to say the same thing with intensity. "Come on, Papi! Let's go!" I don't know why, but the hunger of his words set a good tone for me. I was so curious about who the fan was that I asked the Red Sox to find out his name. I learned that he was Dennis Drinkwater, a Boston business-man in the glass-replacement industry. I knew if Game 3 came down to a key at-bat, I was going to be looking for Dennis before digging in at the plate.

It didn't seem necessary as we cruised through six innings. We led 6–1, and there was no reason to think we'd blow a lead like that in the final three innings. But the Angels got to us in the top of the seventh. They forced us to use four pitchers in the inning, with their biggest hit being a grand slam from league MVP Vladimir Guerrero. His slam tied the score at 6. For a while, it looked like the Angels were going to take the lead in the top of the ninth. They loaded the bases with one out against our new, dominant closer, Keith Foulke. He got out of the jam with consecutive strikeouts. We went quickly in the ninth, so it was on to extra innings.

In the bottom of the 10th, the Angels had gone to their fourth pitcher of the night, a 22-year-old kid named Francisco Rodríguez. He was a talented pitcher, an All-Star, and had one of the highest strikeout rates in baseball. For some reason, I saw the ball well when I faced him. I knew that if I came up against him in the 10th, he'd be taken out and Angels manager Mike Scioscia would likely bring in a lefty to deal with me. Rodríguez gave up a leadoff single to Johnny Damon, but he followed with getting Mark Bellhorn to ground out and surprising Manny with strike three looking.

I was up next.

Just as I'd thought, Rodríguez was removed from the game and replaced by the Angels' Game 1 starter, left-hander Jarrod Washburn. I'd gone back and forth with Washburn over the years. I considered him a power lefty in the sense that although he was consistently be-tween 92 and 94 miles per hour on his fastball, I felt like he threw a heavy ball. He seemed to throw a lot of fastballs that would tail away from me, on the outside of the plate. So, as my friend Dennis was encouraging me to hit and the fans along the lines were rhythmically banging the green walls in anticipation of something big, I made up my mind. As soon as I saw Washburn emerge from the bullpen, I knew I was right. I was going to look for a pitch away and drive it.

With certain pitchers I've faced over the years, I just feel confident that I'm going to do some damage. A few of them, like my boy David Wells, are friends of mine. Kevin Brown was someone I felt that way about. And so was Washburn. My confidence level was already high because of the season I'd had, and the atmosphere at Fenway pushed it somewhere else. I've always been amazed at people who criticize baseball players for showing emotion, especially in playoff games. What do they expect when every move you make is with the game on the line? You're a competitor. You want to be successful for your team and your city. You're not supposed to respond when everyone is losing their minds in the stands, to the point where you really can't hear anything?

Why not?

I wasn't going to overthink anything against Washburn. I was sticking with my plan. He threw what I expected him to, and I instantly recognized the rotation of a fastball fading away from me. The only thing I didn't predict was that the ball caught slightly more of the plate than Washburn wanted. I was relaxed as I put a good swing on it, and I knew it was gone as soon as I made contact. It soared toward and then over the Green Monster, and all those individual conversations I mentioned merged into a mass of sound. I lifted my right hand into the air and kept it that way for a while as I rounded the bases. My teammates were at home plate waiting for me, and we all celebrated with group jumping and hugging, with the plate underneath us somewhere.

It didn't seem like any fan left the park. I could hear some of them yelling and some of them trying to sing along to "Dirty Water," the Fenway anthem after wins. My favorite line in there is *"Boston, you're my home!"* That's exactly what it had become for me. I thought Pedro had lost it that day in the Dominican when, outside of a restaurant, he cheered when I told him that I had been released by Minnesota. He explained later that he was excited because he knew I had a chance to play with him in Boston. I spotted Pedro as I stood on the field after the walk-off, and there was a wide smile and pure joy on his face. He was right. This was better than anything I'd experienced in baseball. We had won the game and the series, and now there was just a short wait for what I'd planned an entire year for. I knew we'd have another chance to take on the Yankees for the pennant, and here we were. I was certain that it wouldn't end like it had the previous season.

I enjoyed everything about playing in New York. It was abnormal, but in a good way. There were more lights and cameras than normal. More broadcasters and reporters, speaking English and Spanish, asking more questions than normal. There were more people in the park, which could seat 20,000 more fans than Fenway. As a left handed hitter, I imagined what it would be like to play half of the games with a fence so close in right field, just over 300 feet away.

All around us in the stands were famous actors, rappers, and entertainers. And across from us on the field was a team of remarkable players who I knew even then would be in the Hall of Fame one day. Derek Jeter. Mariano Rivera. Alex Rodriguez. Gary Sheffield. Mike Mussina. The manager, Joe Torre, would be a Hall of Famer too. I loved the history of the park, and even the sound of it. The public address announcer was a man named Bob Sheppard. I'd never seen him, but from his voice I pictured him as a precise, elegant gentleman in no hurry to get anywhere. I couldn't get enough of the entire production. I loved the competition between us and the Yankees, but I can't lie and say I didn't also love all the attention. I counted on it. I felt stronger knowing that I could help my team win a game while everyone in the world, it seemed, was watching.

Despite my affection for New York, we couldn't get out of there quickly enough after the first two games of the championship series. In Game 1, we learned just how bad Schilling's ankle was. He didn't look like himself in the opener and lasted just three innings. Baseball writers from around the country reported that he needed surgery. Baseball commentators suggested that the potential loss of Schilling for the series would be too much for us to overcome. In Game 2, Pedro pitched well. The problem was that the Yankees' starter, Jon Lieber, pitched one of the sharpest and most consistent games of his life. Our offense, the best in baseball, was held to a run.

I didn't detect any fear or doubt from my teammates. We were going back to Fenway, where we didn't just win games — we wore people out there. We won more than two-thirds of our home games, and I think our family approach had a lot to do with it. It wasn't just the players. Tiffany had dozens of best friends among the players' wives and girlfriends and used to call Trot Nixon's wife, Katherine, a saint. Tiffany knew that if we weren't hanging out with Pedro and his family, Johnny Damon and his wife, Michelle, were likely doing something for the team at their house. There was Jeanna Millar, Dawn Timlin . . . so many great families. We were together all the time, and I think that closeness put the focus on fun and kept us out of any long-term arguments or any other foolishness. Any kind of foolishness going on with the team was by design; I guess that's why one of our nicknames was "The Idiots."

I knew we'd score some runs and get back in the series. But on one of the strangest nights of my career, the opposite happened. And I'll admit it: I was crushed. Game 3 had begun as if it would turn into one of those classics that's decided in the ninth inning. Or extra innings. Instead, it was probably over in the fifth, when the Yankees led 13–6. Maybe we knew we couldn't win it in the seventh, when it was 17–8. At the end of the night, it was New York ahead by the embarrassing score of 19–8.

Listen, I don't care what anyone tells you now. When you're down three games in a best-of-seven series with the Yankees, you're not thinking, *Hey, we're going to come back and win this shit.* That's fiction. They had put up fireworks the game before with 19 runs, and it was our third straight loss to them. I'd be a straight-up bullshitter if I told you I was thinking we could win the series. I wanted to play the game the right way and not get swept. They had just kicked our ass, and they were an incredible team. They had a lot of confidence in themselves. I didn't see any reason to say they were going to collapse and we were going to come back. The only person who said that was my friend Kevin Millar, but of course *he* would say that — Millar doesn't have a brain.

Seriously, as we headed to Game 4 at Fenway, we didn't want to leave the fans with this thought of us. Not only did I know what our fans would say about us if we got swept, I knew what would be said to them by New Yorkers. There were New Yorkers and Yankees hats all over Boston. If we allowed the Yankees to send us home, at home, their smirks would be there permanently. There would also be more changes. More trades. More negative commentary about baseball in Boston and doubts about our ability to win a World Series in our lifetimes.

We did a good job of keeping some drama in the series. It was competitive in the bottom of the ninth in Game 4, but we trailed by a run, 4–3. The Yankees brought out their weapon, the opponent I respected the most in my career: Mariano Rivera, who had saved 53 games in the regular season. I thought he was brilliant, and that had nothing to do with his saves or his sub-two ERA. He threw one pitch, a cutter, over and over, and yet hitters couldn't figure him out. My batting average was okay against him, but I never felt that I crushed any of his pitches. He could make your life miserable.

The sellout crowd at Fenway was standing when Mariano began

the ninth by pitching to Millar. I've known Millar since we were both in the minors, and I can tell you he's been a comedian his entire life. He's one of the funniest people I've ever met in baseball. But he knew baseball, and he could be businesslike when he needed to. I loved his approach against Mariano. He worked a leadoff walk, which allowed us to bring in pinch-runner Dave Roberts. Roberts was a fast and daring base runner, and as soon as he got on the field, he started distracting Mariano by taking a huge lead. When he decided to run, it seemed he would get to second easily. But the catcher, Jorge Posada, made a great throw to second. Anyone else on our team probably would have been out. Roberts, though, slid his left hand into second base just before Derek Jeter made a swipe at him for the tag.

Safe.

The crowd had been with us all night, and now they were louder than they had been in that series clincher against the Angels. They wanted so much right there, and we could all feel it. It all came down to one thing: they were tired of being embarrassed by the Yankees. That was true of this series, the 2003 series, the 1999 series, and all the way back through history. I wanted to give them something special, but first we just needed to push across a run. Bill Mueller was at the plate, and he singled up the middle to bring home Roberts. It was 4–4 and we had a chance.

I could have broken that tie with two outs and the bases loaded in the ninth. Mariano was a master, and I could feel that he had me off balance. He got me to pop up to second, and that threat was over. I knew if I could get another opportunity, we'd win it. I respected so many of their pitchers, but I knew Mariano wouldn't be in the game my next at-bat. I liked my percentages against anyone who wasn't him.

In the 12th inning, that man turned out to be Paul Quantrill.

He was the perfect example of why I stayed up late at night in the off-season, thinking about pitchers. I had watched a lot of video on Quantrill, who had pitched for Boston years before and who had one of the toughest pitches to identify in the game. It was a front-door sinker, and he'd gotten me out with it before. Nasty pitch. It starts off coming right at you, and you think it's going to hit you. If you don't know the pitch, you'll give up on it. But if you anticipate it, you know it comes toward you and then sinks back over the plate. What makes it even trickier is that some pitchers throw a cutter with that same action. So it's easy to get confused and think the cutter is the sinker. That's an easy way to get jammed and pop up.

I had seen that video, though, and I didn't remember Quantrill ever throwing me a cutter. I was sitting sinker. As I went to the plate, with Manny already on first, I was thinking, *Come on, give it to me.* I didn't want to just make contact. My mentality was that I needed to hit it out. He threw that front-door sinker and I was ready for it. Kind of. The pitch he threw was excellent. It started more inside than I thought it would, so for a split second it gave the illusion of hitting me. Then, although I knew it was coming back over the plate, it came back more inside than middle. I was fortunate, though. I got ahold of the pitch, and as it flew over the outfield and into the right-field stands, I was immediately grateful for the payoff of hard work. I knew I could do something like that again, and so could my teammates. Finally, it was a real series.

The next day I recognized our team again. We were The Idiots. We were laughing and telling jokes. I noticed the difference in our attitude from the moment I walked into the park. I think there was relief that we weren't going to get swept, but there was no satisfaction in winning just a game. If the Yankees were going to win the series, at least we could stop them from celebrating on our field. It was on, and you could feel it even with the National Anthem. Our fans were even more intense than the night before, and *that* had been the wildest crowd I'd ever seen and heard.

In the eighth inning, we were in a similar position as the night before. This time we trailed 4–2, and I was facing another former Red Sox pitcher: Tom "Flash" Gordon, one of the most difficult relievers to plan for. He had a fantastic breaking ball that went twelve o'clock to six o'clock, a big looper that messed with your timing. And if you looked for it too much, Flash threw a 97-mile-per-hour fastball that could shut you down. We battled in the eighth until I got a hitter's count and guessed that he would have to throw me a fastball. I hit it over the Green Monster to make it 4–3, and Jason Varitek hit a sacrifice fly to tie it at 4.

The score stayed tied for hours — literally. When we got to the 14th inning, the game, amazingly, had passed the five-and-a-half-hour mark, and I was facing a pitcher named Esteban Loaiza. The two teams had used 14 pitchers in the game. Anyone who stayed in the park or stayed up to watch the game on TV could feel the desperation. Down 3–1 in the series, we were feeling desperate for obvious reasons, but the Yankees were feeling it too, and they probably shouldn't have. They had control of the series. But as the game extended past midnight and they saw our fight, I think they started to get nervous about what they had awakened. The next night in New York I would see those nerves, and it would be because of what happened in that 14th. With Manny and Johnny Damon on base, I worked Loaiza for a game-winning single.

My teammates swarmed me again, just as they had at the end of Game 4. Friends of mine and media members alike wanted to know what I was feeling. Nervous? Excited for the pressure situation? Neither. I was 28 years old, and we were playing the Yankees for a chance to go to the World Series. I felt blessed to be a part of it. I just wanted to return to New York.

As we prepared for Game 6, I looked at the Yankees and saw that they didn't have that superhero pose that they usually had in the dugout. I wasn't the only one who noticed it. They were tight. And we knew that feeling because we'd had it ourselves from the middle of Game 3 until the final out of Game 4. Now, before the start of the sixth game, we felt that we were ahead in the series although we were down three games to two.

Positive things started to happen for us, beginning with Schilling, who probably shouldn't have been pitching. He'd torn tendons in his right ankle, and the medical team had done what it could to stabilize them. But the fix was temporary, and you could see the blood seeping through his right sock as he stood on the mound. He picked us up more than I or anyone else dreamed he would, and after seven miraculous innings in which he gave up a single run, we were in position to be where we were the year before: in New York for a chance to win the pennant.

In New York, I decided that everything didn't have to be like the previous year. Then, I'd managed just two hours of sleep as I locked myself in my Times Square hotel room and refused to relax. Not this time. A few of my friends were in town, and after the game we went for a late-night meal in Queens. We went to Café Rubio, ordered all sorts of delicious Dominican food and red wine, and sat in a private room in the back.

We were having a great time, telling stories, laughing, and drinking. It was starting to get late, and one of my boys suggested that we leave. I guess I had been enjoying myself more than I thought, because I was tipsy. As I walked through the restaurant I saw a few Yankees fans sitting near the front who recognized me and playfully teased me in Spanish.

"*Estas borracho?*" they asked, laughing.

They wanted to know if I was drunk.

"How are you supposed to be ready for Game 7 when you're here like this?"

We exchanged a few one-liners, and then I pointed to the big-screen TV on the wall.

"I want you guys to be here tomorrow to watch the game," I told them. "I'm going to hit a home run."

They laughed and said they'd be there, and we left. They didn't realize that I always felt at ease against Kevin Brown, the Game 7 starter. They didn't know how relaxed our team was. And as I'd see myself before the start of the final game, they didn't know just how uncomfortable the Yankees were with the position they were in. I have a friend who works for a Spanish-language newspaper in New York, and he had gone to the New York clubhouse a couple of hours before first pitch.

"You guys are about to whup that ass tonight," he told me.

I asked him why he put it that way.

"Because when I went over there, it was like a funeral. And over here, it's like you guys are ready for a party."

We were. We were overdue. It happened quickly too. In the first inning, Johnny Damon got on base, stole second, and tried to score on a sharp single to left by Manny. But Johnny hesitated going from second to home, and he was thrown out at the plate. As Yankee Stadium continued to buzz over the play, I swung at the first pitch I saw from Brown and smashed it to right. It left the park fast, and we were up 2–0 in the first. By the second, Brown was out of the game. He turned the game over to Javier Vázquez, who entered with the bases loaded. Johnny was ready for him. He hit a grand slam, which pushed the lead to 6–0.

There was no chance of us blowing a lead on this night. It was an accomplishment simply to force a Game 7, and now we were running away with it. Whether we wanted to or not, we were aware of the history that was being made. No team had ever been down 0–3, only to come all the way back to tie and win the series. We heard about the reports in Boston, how people had gathered in bars and at house parties, how they spilled out into the streets when the game was over. My friend Rubio told me that my trash-talkers from the night before did come back to his café to watch Game 7. And when they saw me hit a home run, they told him that I could have dinner there, on them.

But that wasn't the reward I was looking for. After an agonizing off-season, we had beaten the Yankees and taken the pennant. We knew that we still had to play the World Series. Yet on October 20, 2004, it already felt like we'd won it.

When I was a Seattle Mariners prospect in Appleton, Wisconsin, my confidence was remarkably high. On and off the field. One life-changing night I approached a local young woman and said, "Do you have a boyfriend? No? Well, you do now." *Brad Krause / Krause Sports Photography*

Five years after the first flight of my life, I was in the majors as a Minnesota Twin. That's where I first learned a tough lesson: the wrong manager can make your life miserable. *Jed Jacobsohn / Getty Images*

I developed some lifelong relationships with Twins players, but the organization never saw me in the same way that I saw myself. *The Sporting News / Getty Images*

Pedro's persistence paid off: he said he thought I could be the team's next everyday first baseman. He was right. Almost.
Craig Jones / Getty Images

In 2003, I knew that all I needed was a chance to prove myself. I got it in Boston and finished fifth in the MVP race.
Jonathan Daniel / Getty Images

I had a new team in the spring of 2003. With Manny Ramírez, I also had the most demanding workout partner and batting coach of my career. *Boston Globe* / Getty Images

Opposing pitchers began to dread the middle of our lineup, and sights like this became common.
Boston Globe / Getty Images

During the height of our rivalry with the Yankees, it was hard to keep your eyes on one thing. As I'm trying to hold back Manny, New York bench coach Don Zimmer is starting to charge toward Pedro Martínez.
New York Daily News Archive / Getty Images

Our battles against the Yankees, like this one in the 2003 American League Championship Series, were lengthy and exhausting.
Jed Jacobsohn / Getty Images

Pedro Martínez, the smartest teammate I ever had, deserved better for his efforts in Game 7 of the 2003 ALCS. As I sat next to him that night, I began to realize just how different it was to be a member of the Red Sox.
Boston Globe / Getty Images

In 2003, Pedro helped me talk my way into the starting lineup. One year later, our celebratory actions spoke louder than our words.
Jim Rogash / Getty Images

The All-Star Game was nothing new to Manny Ramírez in 2004. But for me, the gala in Houston was the first of my career.
Steve Grayson / Getty Images

Our 2004 team was affectionately nick-named "The Idiots." It was my second family, and players like Johnny Damon always found a reason for a family celebration.
Julie Cordeiro / Boston Red Sox

I've never felt pressure in a baseball game. Not once. It's part of the reason this became routine in October 2004. Julie Cordeiro / Boston Red Sox

I knew New England was passionate about baseball, but I still didn't think we would inspire over 3 million people to attend our 2004 World Series parade.
Cindy M. Loo / Boston Red Sox

My new manager in 2004, Terry "Tito" Francona, impressed me with his willingness to back away from the spotlight. We helped change the way generations of Red Sox fans thought by beating the Yankees for the 2004 pennant.
Doug Pensinger / Getty Images

Theo Epstein, our general manager, listened when I told him that I needed to play. When it came to contracts, though, we didn't always see things the same way.
Charles Rex Arbogast / AP Photo

I had talked with Pedro Martínez enough to understand how much this World Series game meant to him; he knew it was going to be his last start for the Red Sox.
Rich Pilling / Getty Images

In my prime, I learned to be better at weight training and also to recognize pitches. As a result, the game slowed down for me.
Jack Maley / Boston Red Sox

I was happy that Pedro was rewarded with a lucrative contract for the 2005 season. I was crushed that he had to go to the New York Mets to get it. Jim McIsaac / Getty Images

Our 2007 team was a perfect blend of experience and youth. We spent the entire season in first place. Jack Maley / Boston Red Sox

I've never had a teammate like Dustin Pedroia, who goes to sleep and wakes up with baseball on his mind. He gave our entire clubhouse a boost in 2007. Jim Rogash / Getty Images

We found our 2007 playoff identity by erasing Cleveland's commanding series lead in the ALCS. By the time we got to the World Series against Colorado, we were a charging machine that couldn't be stopped. Nick Laham / Getty Images

What a great night it was in
Denver: cancer survivor Jon
Lester won the game, enabling
us to win the World Series.
Christian Petersen / Getty Images

I'll always remember this night
in Denver, when we completed
our World Series sweep of the
Colorado Rockies. There was
beer and champagne here.
Later, there was singing in the
hotel lobby.
Al Tielemans / Getty Images

Nothing compared to
playing in Boston, especially
when the season ended
with a parade.
Cindy Loo / Boston Red Sox

8

Parade Route and Out

I never considered myself a student of history. That is, until I moved to Boston.

Tiffany has always been our family's history buff, with a curiosity about how and when places came to be. That was one of the things that got her excited about Boston when we made the move at the beginning of 2003. She knew there would be plenty to discover in one of America's oldest cities. When I would leave for the park, Tiffany and Alex would explore the city and see many of the historic landmarks for which New England is known.

One of those places is Fenway Park. I guess I never made the connection between Boston baseball and Boston history. I'm not just talking about the legendary men who played for the Red Sox over the years. I'm talking about how much baseball matters to Boston and all of New England. It's more than just a game there. It's tradition. It's community. It's family. I had heard people say all of those things when I signed with the Red Sox, and I had begun to see just how deep that connection was when we lost to the Yankees in 2003.

I had been devastated, and so were the fans. But their devastation was different than mine. I was hurting, and that made me look forward to the next year, to the future. Their hurt, though, took them back to the past. They didn't just carry their own pain. They brought along the disappointed hopes of their parents and grandparents, aunts and uncles, siblings and friends. They looked forward only cautiously, because of past losses to the Yankees and others.

When we returned to Boston after winning the 2004 pennant in New York, I couldn't believe what I was seeing and hearing. The old city had fresh energy. Even though the New England Patriots had set an NFL record for consecutive wins, most people didn't want to talk about them. And even though the Red Sox were going to be hosting the first game of the World Series, against the St. Louis Cardinals, that wasn't the main reason for the lightness in the late October air either. It was all about beating the Yankees, a rare event for the Red Sox with the pennant at stake.

They hadn't come close in the 1920s and 1930s, when the Yankees appeared in 11 World Series and won eight of them. The Sox had finished ahead of the Yankees in 1946, and just behind them in 1949. Between 1950 and 1966, the Yankees participated in 13 more World Series, and won eight of those. The Red Sox were never a threat to knock them off. Boston went to the Series in 1967 and 1975, losing both in seven games. In 1978, there was a one-game playoff at Fenway against the Yankees. New York won it. Boston was in the 1986 World Series and was one strike away from winning. Instead, the New York Mets won that game and the next one for the Series. In 1999, the Red Sox had the fight to beat the Yankees in the league championship series, but not the talent. Then there was 2003 and, finally, our comeback in 2004.

I listened to the radio and heard how excited people were about what we had done. Some people bragged, but they weren't the majority. Instead, most fans had a personal story to tell. Those missed opportunities had gotten into their hearts and heads, and many of them had allowed themselves to believe that the Yankees would never be beaten. When it happened, I heard some people say that they wished their grandpa or grandma had been alive to see it. There was joy in some of those voices and relief in all of them. Years of negativity had begun to melt away. It wasn't just on the radio. It was in letters written to us and to newspapers. It was in conversations around the region, from grocery stores to churches.

Our comeback, our *historic* comeback, was perfect. No one would have believed the story if you had told them, so I'm glad it played out the way it did. The ending in 2003 made the ending in 2004 twice as good. Although some Red Sox fans refused to breathe until the World Series was officially over, many celebrated as if we'd already won it. I was with the fans on that one. It was hard to blame them for assuming the Cardinals were a footnote to such an incredible story. How could we lose after all that momentum and four straight wins? We'd had to be not only perfect but lucky in those four games against the Yankees, and we were both.

I'm usually the kind of person who "gets it" late. It's just the way my brain works. I get so caught up in the moment that it takes me a while to appreciate what's taken place and what it all means. But I wasn't like that before the World Series. I personally felt unstoppable coming off that Yankee series, where I was named the Most Valuable Player. Our team was also hot. The special part about it was that we were playing the best baseball of our careers and having more fun playing baseball than we had ever had. I had never been so close to winning it all, including my time in the minors. It was a high.

Meanwhile, the Cardinals had a solid team. They had won 105 games in the regular season, and their lineup was stacked. Their pitching was good, even if they didn't have anyone who could match up with Pedro and Curt Schilling. Our advance scouts were confident that we could shut them down in the World Series with a smart approach, but we knew that already. They weren't going to beat us four times, especially with us having home-field advantage for the first time in the playoffs.

They made it interesting in a wild Game 1, though. Their starting pitcher was Woody Williams, and even before I got to the plate in the first inning, I could tell he was having a tough time with his grip and location. Manny was batting ahead of me, and with two on, he just missed crushing a homer to right field. It took an amazing play by Larry Walker to catch the ball and keep the game scoreless. But when I got up, Williams let a pitch slip to the inside of the plate and I pulled it to right. I was trying to hit it out, and that's what happened. We got four runs in the first and eventually took a 7–2 lead. But we had four errors in the game, and St. Louis tied it twice late before we finished them off, 11–9.

We had Schilling going in Game 2, and he took away all drama. He didn't give up an earned run. We won, 6–2, our sixth consecutive playoff win. I don't believe any of the guys said it out loud, but we knew it was going to be our last game of the season at Fenway. Pedro and Derek Lowe, both free agents, were scheduled to pitch the next two games.

I hadn't let it sink in yet that Pedro was a few weeks away from possibly being my ex-teammate. He had gone out of his way to recruit me to Boston and to make me and my family comfortable. I owed him so much that I couldn't even begin to put it in words. I was torn. I wanted him to get as much money as he could on the open market, as much as he deserved. I was starting to understand that the Red Sox didn't do things like that. It seemed to me that the team was willing to spend big money, at market value or beyond, on players who had never played in Boston. But there always seemed to be a contract dispute with players who had done well here and proven that they could handle the environment.

Pedro made his start look easy. The Cardinals ran into a couple of outs early in the game, blowing their chance to make Pedro struggle. He pitched seven scoreless innings and gave up three hits. He got all he needed in the first when another player he recruited, Manny, hit a home run. A lot of people don't realize that in 1999 Manny had approached Pedro and told him that there was a good chance he'd be leaving Cleveland. He told Pedro to let the Boston general manager at the time, Dan Duquette, know about his interest. Just over a year later, Manny made the surprising decision to leave Cleveland and sign with the Red Sox.

One game away from winning the Series, everyone in Boston, including the front office, was happy to still have Manny in town. He had played well all year, and the fans had become attached to him. The same could be said for all of us. The Red Sox had been popular long before we all arrived, but now we had a chance to change the way people thought about the team. We weren't the unlucky Red Sox. We weren't making people angry and causing them to lose confidence and hope. We were one good game away from being described as the most significant champions in the history of New England.

As for the last game, honestly, it's one of the few times when the details didn't stick with me. I don't know how long the game was, officially, but it seemed to stretch through the entire night. I just wanted it to be over. I wanted to hug as many people as I could, dance with them, spray a bunch of them with champagne. I felt so blessed. I was on a team that would never be forgotten, and I was playing in a region where they never got tired of talking about and watching baseball. Of course, every player dreams of winning the World Series. But it's even better when you get there, you're one game away from winning it, and you're reflecting on all the steps it took to get there. I had dreamed of getting to the Series before, but I'd never known how to do it. There are so many elements involved. Having talented teammates who also like to have fun. Having the right ownership and management. Working your ass off every day during the season and in the off-season too. Having a little luck.

We had it all in 2004. I've never laughed so hard. I've never been a part of games that lasted so long and meant so much to literally millions of people. I'd always had confidence in my abilities, but I didn't realize that being on the right team, in the right city, with the always engaged Boston fans, could push me to be this kind of player. I was 28 years old, and I felt like my best baseball was in front of me.

The season was now in the past. After Keith Foulke got Edgar Rentería to ground the ball back to him, Foulke tossed the ball to Doug Mientkiewicz. For some people, that was just the formality before the celebration on the mound. For me, it was an intersection. Past and present. Doug knew me before anyone in New England knew my name. He was there in the Twin Cities when we were both a bundle of potential. Tiffany used to joke that the Twins wanted Doug to be me, and me to be Doug. More power from one, more Gold Glove defense from the other. What we both were, on a beautiful Wednesday night in St. Louis, was World Series champions.

I thought we'd never leave the field. There were cameras all around, some belonging to New England TV stations and some from Hollywood. There was a movie, *Fever Pitch*, being made about the Red Sox. It was a romantic comedy and the two stars, Jimmy Fallon and Drew Barrymore, were on the field. My story seemed to have movie elements, but it was real. I got close to Tiffany, and we shared a kiss. There was no need to say much more than that. We knew how much it meant to both of us.

At 3:30 in the morning, our flight from St. Louis departed for Boston. I remember a few guys playing cards on the plane, and Schilling made everyone laugh by making an announcement like a pilot. The one thing I'll never forget is seeing Pedro snuggling with the World Series trophy. The plan was for our oldest teammate, 40-year-old Ellis Burks, to carry it off the plane once we landed, but during the flight it was Pedro's. It seemed to belong there next to him. But this was his next-to-last official act with the Red Sox. In a couple of days there would be a baseball parade and then, finally, he'd be gone.

. . .

As expected, the parade was memorable. My only regret is that I didn't record it. This is going to sound silly, but I didn't know there were so many people in New England. The crowd estimate was 3.2 million. All I can tell you is that the only land I saw was the road the Duck Boats drove on. Otherwise, it was people. Everywhere. They seemed to be piled on top of each other. I tried to wave to everyone, which was impossible. I saw dozens of signs from men and women and boys and girls, of all shapes and sizes and colors. They had pictures of their deceased relatives, with tributes. I saw thousands and thousands of smiles, as well as some tears of joy.

I had promised myself that I would never forget the long faces of defeat after the 2003 loss to New York. I'll never forget the 2004 parade faces either. They were the people who had scheduled their summers around Red Sox games and were always hopeful that there would be playoff games in the fall. I was glad to see them finally get the reward. It's always nice to see a crowd having a good time, and that's all the entire day was about. When the Duck Boats got into the water, there were fans waving on a bridge above the Charles River, and there were even some who jumped in to swim after the boats. I'm not much of a sailor, but I got behind the wheel of the boat and steered for a while.

It would have spoiled the day if we had announced that it was going to be our last time together as a team. But that's exactly what it was: a team breakup party, and one that happened to have a championship trophy along for the ride.

New England felt entitled to that trophy, so it went on tour for the rest of the year. It made several stops around the region and even made it to the Dominican. That was the positive news. Unfortunately, Mets general manager Omar Minaya had made it there before the trophy. He was visiting Pedro, and he asked him directly what it would take to get him on the Mets. Pedro told him that his desire was to stay in Boston. For the Mets to have a chance, their deal needed to be four years guaranteed. They shook hands and said they had a deal, contingent on Boston having an opportunity to match it.

It was going to be the kind of contract that the Red Sox believed they couldn't match. Pedro, five years older than me, felt he couldn't pass it up. It could well turn out to be the last contract of his career, so he had to take the best deal. With all the focus on Pedro, Lowe signed with the Los Angeles Dodgers in a much quieter departure.

The 2005 season was going to be strange at work with no Lowe and no Pedro, but as Tiffany pointed out to me, it was going to be even worse at home. Just like everyone else, we admired Pedro the player. But we loved the person even more. Pedro was still family, of course. Just a family member who was leaving Boston for New York.

9

Life After the Series

The words from my agent were clear and to the point.

"If you wait one more year and go to free agency," he said, "I can easily get you a $100 million contract. There's always going to be a market for a guy like you."

It was early 2005, and we were the defending World Series champions. It was the perfect time to be associated with the Red Sox. That's why there were books, movies, documentaries, and TV shows devoted to the team. It's why the owners excitedly shared their plans to update Fenway Park: new restaurants, new seats in left and right fields, new office space. It's why fans constantly competed to buy the most expensive tickets in baseball, in person and online, guaranteeing another full season of a sold-out Fenway. In my agent's opinion, it was my time to strategize, be patient, and wait for that $100 million windfall.

I was tempted.

I was already outperforming my contract, and my agent knew that it wouldn't be long before the Red Sox started talking about an extension. It would be good business for them, a move that would help them avoid competing for free agents who were commanding spiraling salaries. I was entering my third season with the Red Sox, and I had already seen my share of contract disputes. When I got to town, Nomar Garciaparra was the organization's most important home-grown superstar. He was gone just over a year later after the team presented him with a $60 million contract offer, withdrew it, and eventually traded him. Pedro was one of the best pitchers in Red Sox and baseball history. He got the contract he deserved in free agency, but he had to go to the Mets to get it. Derek Lowe and Orlando Cabrera, two clutch players in October, were off to other teams. And one of the cofounders of The Idiots, Johnny Damon, was in the final year of his contract and unsure if his future was in Boston or elsewhere.

For me, someone who grew up in a family that struggled to earn money, I looked at it this way: if I couldn't make it with the $65 million over five years that the Red Sox eventually offered, I wasn't going to make it with $100 million either. That's not to say I didn't want more money, or didn't think I deserved it. I understood how much I had done for the Red Sox and how much they had done for me. I didn't think it was the time to be gauging my market value. I knew I'd be able to take care of my wife and kids forever, and extending my Red Sox contract would remove any negotiating worries during the season. What I didn't immediately realize, though, was how much my life had changed.

One of the many things I love about Tiffany is that she's never wanted anyone to do for her what she can do for herself. She values being low-key and as normal as possible. You'll never see her with a nanny to look after the kids and shuttle them to their activities. She's always been the one to do that, and she likes it that way. Fame was something that sneaked up on both of us, and we weren't all that prepared for it.

We had moved to a house in Newton, right in the center of town, and our address had been listed in the city's free newspaper. After all the big hits and the World Series, we noticed more and more cars driving ever so slowly by the house. Sometimes people would pull over and point. It was like we were an unofficial stop on the Duck Boat tour. Just after the Series, on Halloween, we passed out candy to the neighborhood kids. Several days later, we'd still have people knocking on the door with late trick-or-treat requests . . . or just to say hello.

We couldn't be anonymous like we were when we first met, nearly ten years earlier. For that matter, we couldn't be anything like we were when we first moved to Boston just two years earlier. We were in a position that we'd never thought of before: How were we going to raise our kids, and spend our time, as a celebrity family? The question itself would have been a joke in Minnesota. Celebrity? No one at the bar across the street from the Metrodome looked at me like that. No one thought about where I lived, what kind of opinions I had, and which social event I'd attended. There, ESPN wasn't wondering if we could tape a commercial, and the late-night talk shows didn't ask about my availability. Fans in New England are passionate about athletes, especially the stars, and now I was considered one of them. A star. It was fine with me, although I was warned that stardom would include not just more visibility, endorsements, and commercials but also consequences.

Manny pulled me aside and told me about being a great player in Boston. "Papi, once you put up unbelievable numbers here, people will never let you change the menu," he said. "You'll always be expected to give them exactly what you've given before."

It would be several years before I could truly appreciate the wisdom of what he'd said. In 2005, I knew I wouldn't have to worry about my numbers falling off. I'd trained hard in the off-season again. I was more knowledgeable about studying pitchers and their tendencies. I've always been big with natural strength, but all the hard workers on the Red Sox inspired me to spend more time in the weight room. I was so mindful of nutrition that I hired a chef just to prepare lunch for me. The year before, I was trying to prove that I could help us win the Series. This year I knew we could win, so the motivation was to win back-to-back.

On the sunny and cool afternoon of our home opener, I was ready for the challenge. I looked around and saw that we were surrounded by some of the most dominant athletes in the history of their sports. As part of our championship gala, the Red Sox had invited local icons, like Bill Russell, Bobby Orr, and Tedy Bruschi, to celebrate with us, but there were also the legends in the visitors' dugout that day. I'm talking about the Yankees. As we received our rings, many Yankees players either applauded us or tipped their caps. I was inspired by the class and dignity many of them showed that day.

It didn't surprise me that the one Yankee who most won over the crowd was Mariano Rivera. When his name was announced, the Fenway fans erupted in applause. It was as if they were teasing him, affectionately, and saying thanks for helping us stay alive in the play-offs. Mariano flashed a big smile when he heard the cheers, and the Boston fans loved him for it.

I'm telling you, I couldn't have more respect for someone as a player and as a man than I do for Mariano. When I made my first All-Star Game, in 2004, I remember watching him walk through the club-house. I viewed him as royalty, but he was so friendly and humble. Anytime he took the mound, he made you appreciate what a talented and smart pitcher he was. For most pitchers, the contact point is out in front of the hitter, where you can see the baseball. For Mariano, the contact point is on your hands. Here's the best way I can describe it: When you're left-handed and standing in the box against Mariano, the baseball makes a big right turn when it comes out of his hand and sometimes the ball is invisible. You see nothing. Then suddenly the ball is right there on your hands. He threw that one pitch, the cutter, but he could do all kinds of things with it, throwing to both lefties and righties. I can tell you now that I used to choke way up on the bat when facing Mariano, just to have a chance of getting a hit.

I learned a lot about believing in myself by watching Mariano. At the beginning of the 2005 season, his velocity was down for some reason, and he had begun to throw changeups and other pitches. Then he must have looked in the mirror one day and asked himself what he was thinking. He went back to the cutter and started dominating again. The lesson there, for me, was to not get too down when going through a hitting slump. To remember who I am and what I do best. Great players need those pick-me-ups too. Once you get to a certain level of achievement, your teammates, coaches, and manager often assume that there's nothing they can tell you to help you. They think you can figure it out on your own. At times, what you need is a simple reminder that you're good and that the skills that made you that way are still in place.

A lot of people wondered if the New England fans' appetite for the Red Sox would shrink after we won the World Series, but I didn't notice it. I could still feel the thick baseball obsession that I loved, at home and on the road. The usual game-by-game scrutiny from the media and fans was still there. But our team, although good, wasn't the same. At the beginning of the year, Curt Schilling wasn't available because of right ankle surgery, and with Pedro and Derek Lowe no longer on the team, that meant that our top two starters along with our number five were gone. The back of our bullpen was different as well. Keith Foulke had done everything right during his first year in Boston. In year two, he didn't look and sound like the same pitcher. He struggled as our closer, and the commentaries from Fenway fans seemed to get under his skin.

I've said it before: playing for the Red Sox isn't for everybody. You've got to have the ability and desire to turn negatives into positives, because the atmosphere is often pessimistic. I liked it when the media told me that I couldn't do something, because I always wanted to come back, prove them wrong, and tell them to shut the hell up. Sometimes I'd say it with more color and nastiness than that. There was nothing they could say or do to intimidate me. I chose to keep things in perspective. I grew up in a neighborhood in Haina where there was a shooting almost every day. Was I going to get shot playing baseball? No. My life was good, even if I went 0-for-4 with three strikeouts. That's just me. Foulke wasn't like that, and neither was our new shortstop, Edgar Rentería. He took some criticism for the way he played, and some for who he wasn't. Cabrera had brought flash and stability to short, and the fans quickly took to his style; Rentería mostly looked uncomfortable. There's no way you can play baseball in Boston — or anywhere — if you give the fans and media power over your performance.

Overall, the year felt strange. From a fan standpoint, there were many reasons to complain about that season. But for the first time in many of their lives, they couldn't link any of our problems to a curse from generations ago. We had won it, so all the talk about the Red Sox not getting it done in the clutch was old and tired. We had trashed that way of thinking with our comeback. We did have some problems, though. Some of them were obvious to me, and others I didn't realize until the season was over. Many championship teams had probably had the same issues we had on the field and in the clubhouse. Guys playing for contracts and wanting more playing time. Somebody being unhappy with their role. Or someone underachieving and losing their everyday job.

I was friends with everyone, so it was hard to see some of the battles. Kevin Millar had been great for us in 2003 and 2004. In 2005, a first baseman named John Olerud started to take some of his playing time. Mark Bellhorn had been our second baseman in 2004, and he'd come up with some key hits. But his strikeouts started to matter more than his on-base capability, so Tony Graffanino and Alex Cora took some of his playing time. Johnny Damon was still playing hard, playing hurt, and giving his entire body to the game. But no one talked contract with him for 2006, even though he desperately wanted to be back. In June, after the amateur draft, there was talk that the team had drafted Johnny's replacement. The kid, from Oregon State, was named Jacoby Ellsbury.

I wish I could say that one thing that remained unchanged was the middle-of-the-lineup power that Manny and I provided. That was half true. There was not a combination like us in baseball, and in any game we knew it was only a matter of time before a pitcher was hurt by one of us, if not both. The problem was that Manny's relationship with management, which had been up and down for years, was down again. I was convinced that he was doing things so they would be forced to trade him. He wouldn't show up when they wanted him to. He didn't always run hard when they wanted him to. Once, Tito asked him to change his off day because Trot Nixon couldn't play, and Manny refused.

Part of it was that Red Sox thing I've described. Some players felt suffocated from all the attention. Manny was living downtown at the time, next to a sports club, and he complained about all the people he had to go through just to go outside. Now, you could ask, "Why didn't he just move somewhere else?" That's a good question. But that wasn't Manny. I think he just wanted a change of scenery, and the Red Sox wanted to give it to him. But by July, they still hadn't found a deal that made sense for them.

Manny stayed, and we put up some incredible numbers, numbers that actually had several voters saying that I could be MVP of the league. I had 47 home runs, 40 doubles, and 148 runs batted in. Manny's numbers were similar in those same categories: 45, 30, and 144. But another player who was having a strong season was Alex Rodriguez. The Yankees had begun the season 11-19, but they'd cleaned themselves up and gotten into position to win the division in the final series of the regular season. That series was against us, at Fenway.

We needed to sweep them to win the division outright. Instead, we won two out of three and finished with 95 wins, the same as the

Yankees. But they became American League East champs when they won the tiebreaker. At least we were headed to the playoffs. And if finishing with the same number of wins was the worst thing that happened to us in 2005, we would be all right. Unfortunately, that *wasn't* the low point of the season. Not even close.

10

In and Out Red Sox

It barely counted as a playoff run, especially after what we had been through the previous two years. We had become known for keeping New England fans awake deep into October with our dramatic baseball games. Night after night. Series after series. Whether we took on the A's or Angels, the Yankees or Cardinals, it was hard to predict what we'd do next.

Until we played the Chicago White Sox in 2005. We didn't go on a long playoff run at all. Instead, we had a short week, and a bad one at that. We lost our first playoff game 14–2. They had a five-run first inning in Game 1, and a five-run fifth inning in Game 2. In Game 3, at Fenway, they beat us another way. They turned the game over to their bullpen for the final four innings and held us to two hits in that span.

Just like that, we were swept out of the playoffs.

The abrupt finish was a good reminder of the kind of business I was in. It's risky to be a long-range planner in any major league city. It's even riskier to do it in the big markets like Boston, New York, Chicago, and Los Angeles. I felt blessed to be married to a woman who instinctively understood that every year either we might have to pack up and go or our friends on the team would have to do it. I didn't think I was going to be traded, but Tiffany's view of things was a good one: be adaptable and ready for anything. From afar, it might seem strange that a so-called superstar would have that view. But I didn't think of myself that way. When I was out in public, I loved the attention, the kind words, signing things for people, taking pictures, and making little kids smile. I also cherished being at home and doing things with the family. I wasn't Papi to them. I think we all kept each other grounded.

Besides, honestly, I was still in awe of things that more experienced stars were used to. I'd never been highly recruited, I'd never made a lot of money, and I'd never been swarmed on the street while taking a walk. I'd been in the big leagues for years and that had never happened. Then, overnight, it did. It blew my mind. I still couldn't believe some of the things that had happened as a result of the Series win. I was originally booked to go on Jimmy Kimmel's show on ABC, but then NBC and *The Tonight Show* wanted me to go on with them instead. NBC and ABC competing for me to come on with them. It got so crazy that Jay Leno made a personal call to one of my agents, saying it would be cool if I came on with him. A *personal* call from Leno? Get the hell out of here! That was nuts.

I was also asked to do my first two endorsements. One was for D'Angelo, a local sandwich shop. The other one was for Comcast. I was honored that someone trusted me enough to make me their spokesman. I took it seriously.

I knew it was going to be a busy off-season. I was 29 and a veteran, so there weren't many things in the game capable of surprising me. For example, I guessed that a few of my boys from the World Series team, Johnny Damon, Kevin Millar, and Bill Mueller, had probably played their final games for the Red Sox. I also had listened to and been around Manny enough to understand that he might ask to be traded, again, at any time.

There was one fight that I didn't see coming, though. It was between Larry Lucchino, president of the Red Sox, and Theo Epstein, the general manager. An in-house war. It was about money and power. It reached the point where Theo decided he didn't want to work for the organization if Larry, and ownership, wouldn't allow him to do his job the way he wanted. He resigned almost one year after we'd been on the field in St. Louis, passing around the World Series trophy.

I found it interesting. I had spent so much time thinking about how the clubhouse would be different without some of our players. It never occurred to me that the GM wouldn't be there.

This all went down at the end of October, close to Halloween. When the media started to figure out what was going on, many of them camped outside of Fenway to get comments from Theo. But he didn't want to talk, so he escaped by putting on a gorilla costume and walking by everyone, unnoticed. I didn't take sides, although I saw the situation for what it was: Theo had the title of GM, but in some ways he was the puppet. He was the shield who took the heat when things went wrong, even if they weren't his decisions. I remember thinking, *Theo manned the fuck up and left town. Wow. That took some balls.* I knew he'd be all right because he was the young executive who had helped the Red Sox win the World Series.

The Theo story was big. With every move, it seemed like the organization was trying to do something even bigger to top it. One of those moves happened around Thanksgiving. We traded a couple of kids in their early twenties, Hanley Ramírez and Aníbal Sánchez, to the Marlins in exchange for Josh Beckett and Mike Lowell. Beckett was a kid himself. He was a 25-year-old ace pitcher, and it made a lot of sense for us to get him. Lowell was a good third baseman with a sizable contract, so he was going to have the job here, not Mueller, in 2006. Kevin Youkilis was going to replace Kevin Millar at first. Just as that news was settling in, it got topped by something else. Johnny left. For the Yankees.

It was hard to watch the team come apart so quickly. When we won it all, we knew that one of the things that made it special was the changing nature of baseball. None of us was crazy enough to think that the whole team could come back and we'd go on a run for a few years. You never think that. But the end never looks and feels the way you think it will. I know for a fact that Johnny wanted to stay with the Red Sox, and I thought it would happen. He did so much for the team, from providing the Idiot look with the long hair and scruffy beard, to seeing a lot of pitches as our leadoff guy, to being prepared to play at all times in any condition.

But realistically, he had to leave. Red Sox fans weren't going to see it that way because he went to the only team they couldn't reasonably understand him going to. But the Yankees guaranteed him $12 million more than the Red Sox did. Playing for that team not only assured him more money and visibility, but meant that he'd be in the playoffs year after year.

There was a lot happening, which was usually the case with Boston baseball. It was easy to get lost in the incredible environment, especially in late 2005 and early 2006. As a prominent member of the Red Sox, I often thought of things from the perspective of the New York–Boston rivalry. The back-and-forth sniping from fans and ownership happened year-round. I never allowed myself to become so intensely involved in it that I couldn't talk to their players or anything like that. But at times I needed to be reminded that the Yankees–Red Sox rivalry wasn't just about baseball. It brought a lot of national and international attention to us all, and we had an opportunity to use that platform in baseball and beyond.

I can't say that I arrived at that revelation on my own. It started to click for me when a family friend told me about the work she was doing. Hearing about it moved me deeply.

She told me about the hospital she worked at in the Dominican, Plaza de la Salud Hospital de Ninos. She was constantly around children who had a variety of heart ailments. When I went to visit, I saw a little boy who brought me to tears. He was about two years old, around the same age as my son. I could barely see his face because it was covered with a mask, and there were tubes and machines all around him. I was overcome with many emotions, including guilt. Why wasn't I doing something to help out here? How could I do more to help in other places? I'm sure that a lot of those kids came from poor families like mine. If we'd had any medical issues when I was growing up, I don't know how my parents could have paid those bills.

That visit to the hospital haunted me. I felt I should have been doing a little extra to try to make things better. I kept thinking, *I wish I knew how to be a better helper . . . all I know is that working with kids is something I love doing.* My problem, at first, was that I didn't know how to ask for help without it being misinterpreted. I wanted no credit whatsoever for what I was doing, but I wanted to lend my name to the cause so I could maximize exposure to bring in money. What was the best way to do that? I believe in God, and I believe that God gave me my talent not just to entertain people by playing baseball but to help those in need. It's not me; it's Him. He's the one who causes people to do good things. I told my agents that I wanted to be thoughtful about a mission. What's the best way to raise awareness and money so we can save lives? That's all I care about. Seeing those sick kids was like seeing members of my own family.

That day the idea for my Children's Fund was born. Did I know what I was doing? Of course not. I had never heard of 501(c)(3)s and 501(a)(3)s. I had a lot to learn about tax codes and the proper umbrellas under which to place charitable giving. But my focus had shifted to using baseball to better lives.

Looking at life from that view made it easier to accept whatever was happening with the Red Sox. I looked at the situation between Theo and Larry and gained a valuable business lesson from it. Nearly three months after resigning from the organization, Theo returned with a new title, more responsibility, and more money. I saw where he was coming from, and I was inspired by his willingness to stick to his principles. I believed that players, if they had the leverage, should do the same thing to get what they'd earned. It wasn't always presented that way in the media when players did it, but you can't let the media or anyone else tell you what your life is supposed to be.

I was happy with our team at the beginning of 2006. We had a new center fielder to replace Johnny, Coco Crisp, and a shortstop, Alex Gonzalez, who took the place of Edgar Rentería. The 2005 season had been tough for Rentería in the field, but that wasn't going to happen with Gonzalez. He was smooth and fluid, one of the best glove men I'd ever seen. I thought our starting pitching would be good with Beckett, Curt Schilling, Tim Wakefield, and Jon Lester, the kid who was almost traded to Texas with Manny Ramírez. There was another reason for excitement, and it was probably part of the reason Theo was lured back to Boston. He said he wanted to mix veterans with prospects from the system. It was time for the prospects to grow up. He probably didn't want that to happen without being around to see it.

There was a young pitcher in the bullpen, Jonathan Papelbon, whose fastball was awesome, and other emerging players in the organization, besides Lester and Papelbon, were just a year or two away from helping us. No matter who they brought in, the lineup was built around Manny and me. I never knew specifically how each season would look, but I was confident that we'd both be all right with us protecting one another.

It wasn't just fun to watch Manny. He was also a great teacher for anyone who wanted to know more about hitting. He always had an understanding of what was going to be thrown at him during the game, and he was prepared for it. If you watched him in batting practice, you saw that he never worked without a plan. His entire workout was based on what he was likely to get in a game.

For me, no matter what I got in the game, the results seemed to be going in the same direction. Up and out. Early in the season, I got into one of those grooves where everything I hit was in the air. I didn't question it. I thought I'd just go with that flow. I'd hit 40-plus home runs the last two seasons. I didn't see any reason why I couldn't hit 50 in 2006.

The first few months of the season didn't go exactly as planned, but it was close. Papelbon took the closer's job from Foulke and was immediately one of the best relievers in the league. Beckett clearly had superior talent, but that's not enough in the American League East. Some National League pitchers are surprised at how deep the lineups are in the AL, and how many hitter's parks there are. Plus, batters quickly adjust to what you're doing. They watch video, talk to teammates, do whatever it takes to figure out what you're doing. At times Beckett struggled with knowing the hitters, and he fought to push his ERA below the high fours most of the summer. But his AL debut was phenomenal, and he dominated batters with his stuff. He had some moxie about him too, and that never hurts.

I had 30 home runs by the All-Star Game, which I made for the third year in a row. Manny had 24 homers and was an All-Star too. Once again, as a team, we were going back and forth with the Yankees atop the division and on our way to the playoffs. At the trading deadline, July 31, we led the East by one game over New York.

Then it was time for the intersection of baseball and real life, with frightening news coming from both directions. It was ironic that it happened on that day, the night of my first Children's Fund event in Boston. The mayor of Boston, my friend Tom Menino, came out to support the fund-raiser at a club called Rumor. It was a modest beginning, and we raised just $75,000, but we were on our way to helping those with heart trouble. The irony was that I was just a few weeks away from being evaluated for heart irregularities myself. As scary as that sounds, it wasn't the most serious issue facing our team. It also wasn't the loss of our captain, Jason Varitek, who was out with a knee injury for five weeks.

After I felt a strange sensation in my chest that was described as "heart palpitations," I spent some time in the hospital and then went back when I felt the same sensation ten days later. After a thorough evaluation, I was given a clean bill of health. But it was no time to celebrate my good news when I heard about Jon Lester. The pitcher, just 22, had swollen lymph nodes, and what was feared turned out to be true. He had cancer — non-Hodgkin's lymphoma.

The season had lost not only its importance but its relevance as well. We started a vicious reverse slide through the standings and ended up far out of playoff contention. Individually, I still continued to crush home runs. I broke the Red Sox record of 50, set by Jimmie Foxx in 1938. I finished with 54. I tied Babe Ruth for number of road homers, at 32. I'm not much for measuring the significance of an achievement as it's happening. What I usually do is take a few weeks or months, sometimes even years, and look back on what's been done. I couldn't do that this time.

You hear so many stories about the history of Fenway, the oldest park in the American League. They've been playing baseball there forever. It made me pause. I'd broken a team record that had stood longer than my father had been alive? And even if it was just for a game, I was in the same sentence as Babe Ruth? I was grateful for everything, individually, that the 2006 season provided.

But the numbers have always been secondary. After we won in 2004, I didn't think that was enough for my career. I wanted more. I was also concerned about my teammates, on and off the field. I wanted to know that Jon Lester was going to be okay. I wanted to know who the organization was going to bring in to replace Trot

Nixon and Mark Loretta, who weren't going to be re-signed to play right field and second base. Of course, there were the annual Manny questions. Did he want to come back? Did they want him to come back?

As more and more players from 2003 and 2004 started to be phased out, I could have made equal arguments for two ways of thinking. One was to anticipate that the same thing that had happened to Pedro and Nomar and Johnny was going to happen to me. The other was to feel empowered as one of the few veterans in the clubhouse who knew what it was like to win in Boston.

I felt empowered.

I knew Theo had spent the fall of 2005 in a front-office dispute that caused him to leave. Now that he had returned, I was hopeful that he and I would see some things the same way. Maybe he'd be willing to talk to me, GM to player, about winning plans for 2007.

II

Coasting

There were several times in my career when I didn't understand what Theo Epstein was thinking and I had no interest in talking with him. It was nothing personal. Theo the smart and passionate Red Sox fan was cool with me. But Theo the numbers-crunching Red Sox executive was a real motherfucker when it came to negotiating my contracts.

I felt like he drove a hard bargain when it came to his own players. When it came to free agents who had no history with the Red Sox, he was likely to keep handing out the cash until they eventually said yes. I didn't like it, but I understood. That's the unfair reality of the free agent market. It's not a time when the best players get paid; it's a time when the best *available* players get paid. I knew it was a system that I couldn't change, but I'd be lying if I said I wasn't pissed about the situation every now and then. I'll tell you what always made me feel better about my big-spending team: we had an opportunity to compete for all the top free agents, and ultimately that gave me a better chance to win a championship.

The end of the 2006 season was one of those times when I didn't mind talking to Theo. And as I talked with him, giving my opinion on what we needed in 2007, I got the feeling that he was genuinely listening to what I had to say. I knew that he had his own thoughts on how to improve a team that didn't crack 90 wins and missed the playoffs for the first time in four years. He was going to fill at least one of our holes, second base, with a rookie named Dustin Pedroia. But when I talked with him, I asked for more pitching.

As long as I had Manny batting behind me, it was going to be hard for any team to deal with our lineup. Manny had gone through another round of trade requests in 2006, and once again the Red Sox had decided that he was too valuable for a swap. It was going to be at least one more year of Manny being Manny in Boston. I told Theo that if we could get another starter and more help in the bullpen, there was no reason why we couldn't get back to the playoffs and the World Series. I didn't think we were that far away.

I felt like I was seeing our team in a similar way to how Theo did. Then he surprised me. It turned out he was seeing players who hadn't even crossed my mind. One of them was a celebrated pitcher from Japan named Daisuke Matsuzaka. There was a lot of hype around him before he ever threw a major league pitch. Because of the multiple pitches and flawless control that he supposedly had, some people had started calling him "the Greg Maddux of Japan."

What made Matsuzaka more intriguing was the process required to sign him. Each interested team had to declare how much it was willing to spend in a blind bid. Brian Cashman, the GM of the Yankees, put in a bid of $33 million. Theo's was $51.1 million. Once again, there was that easy money with players who hadn't proven a thing in Boston. The Red Sox were willing to give up stacks of cash simply to negotiate with him, and they'd have to give up a lot more when it was time for the actual contract. I felt many emotions, all at the same time: awed, unappreciated, hopeful. This is how I can explain that. Awed because the Red Sox and Yankees had combined to bid $84 million on a pitcher who *might* be able to pitch in the big leagues;

unappreciated because I brought more than "designated hitter" to the Red Sox and they knew it, yet at contract time I was just a DH; hopeful because, hey, all would be good with me if we won.

By the time we got to spring training, our spending spree had brought in Dice-K, Julio Lugo, J. D. Drew, J. C. Romero, and Hideki Okajima. The pitchers weren't the only new additions to the staff. There was also a new pitching coach, John Farrell, who had left a front-office job in Cleveland to be on the field daily with Tito Francona, one of his best friends.

Sometimes the spring can tell you right away what kind of chemistry you're going to have as a team. I knew we had a good balance immediately, and I didn't figure it out due to something deep. It was actually our response to silliness that let me know our collective personality was accepting and relaxed. It began with, of all things, a car auction. A story had been going around that Manny, who loved collecting vintage cars, was trying to sell a classic Lincoln Continental. He was scheduled to be at an auction in New Jersey when he was supposed to be at spring training in Florida. Instead of flipping out, it seemed that everyone had some laughs with it, and as it turned out, Manny arrived in camp when he was supposed to.

A month later, Manny was at it again. Once again, the "incident" inspired more comedy than frustration. This time he was putting a gas grill on eBay, along with an autographed baseball. The bids for it didn't approach Dice-K levels, but they went as high as eBay would allow before the gas grill was eventually withdrawn from the site.

We left Fort Myers with smiles, and there wouldn't be many occasions all season that would make us want to change them. I was impressed with a couple of our new players, for completely different reasons. The rookie second baseman, Pedroia, worried me at first. I'd watch him struggle at the plate and think, *Damn, I don't know if he's gonna make it.* There was a stretch in April and May when he went 5-for-42 for a .119 batting average. Then he did something that I've never seen. He went on a 35-for-76 tear, good for a .460 batting average.

I'm not joking: I hadn't seen it before. Every night it would be two hits, three hits, four hits. He was incredible. And I'm not just talking about catching fire. To me, Pedroia is the prototype. I'd never met anyone like him in baseball. It's hard to explain. For example, I love baseball. Love it. But what I saw from Pedroia made it clear to me that his connection to baseball was beyond everyone else's. It was so much more than just love for the game. He *was* the game. Seriously. Everything that was good and true about baseball was in Dustin Pedroia. He breathed it. He lived it. He'd do anything to play it, to be around it, to talk about it. He was such a force of energy, talent, and humor that it lifted our entire clubhouse.

It didn't surprise me that Pedroia was the kind of guy who would play when he was hurt. Eventually, I had to tell him not to. I explained that no one outside of the clubhouse would appreciate his effort, and even if they did, he wasn't helping himself or us by going out there at 60 or 70 percent. Look, the fact that the conversation needed to happen tells you about the commitment to the game the kid had.

Another talented player, totally different from Pedroia, was J. D. Drew. Hold on, because you're going to think I'm just messing around when I tell you this: when J.D. wanted to play, he was the best player I've ever seen. No bullshit. Listen, I said, *when he wanted to play,* he was the best.

The problem was that he could be hot, in a 15-for-20 groove, and you could tell him that you were giving him a couple of days off. He'd take it, without a protest. That's how he was. I don't think he enjoyed being out there every day, but when he wanted to be, he was one of the best ever, both offensively and defensively. He was a five-tool player, and very smart. He was quiet, always reading. Personality-wise, it was like an English teacher had been turned into a baseball player.

He wasn't into any crap, and when we would do our clubhouse pranks, he'd be like, "Oh, come on, man." A great, laid-back guy. But I'll be real with you: some days I wanted to kill him. I had some days when I would say, "Really, you're not going to play because of *that?*" Some days he would come out of the game because his left nut was hurting. It made no sense sometimes, but that's how he was. Theo is a stats guy, and that's why he loved J.D. But the organization had to have known everything about what they were going to get when they gave him $70 million over five years.

As we got deep into the season, though, the only numbers that mattered were the ones that told the story of us and the Yankees. We started having fun in spring training, and by the Fourth of July we had an 11-game lead in the division. Three weeks later, we were in the middle of a stretch of games in which we'd win eight of nine.

But that wasn't the only good news. On July 23, we beat the Indians in Cleveland, and our starter and winner was 23-year-old Jon Lester. He'd worked his way through six chemotherapy treatments to beat cancer and resume his baseball career. He was such a gifted pitcher and sincere person. Our whole team had worried about him the previous September when he'd received his diagnosis. It was inspiring to see him out there, in front of his mom and dad, pitching with such purpose and power. I can tell you, for sure, that this was no ordinary game in July.

Along the way to the playoffs, we had a few moments that stood out.

There was always a question about Manny, and speculation on when he would go through a swoon and not be available to the team for a chunk of time. On August 25, we played a game in New York against the Yankees. We began the night with an eight-game lead in the division, but that wasn't enough to allow us to exhale against a team like New York. Manny hit a home run, his 20th of the season, and drove in a run, his 86th. I also drove in a run that game, number 88 of the season. But then, while my numbers continued to progress during the rest of the baseball season, Manny's stayed right there. He didn't play for the next month due to what he said was a knee injury. With so many fan questions about his commitment over the years, even a legitimate Manny injury was cause for skepticism. The time to check in with Manny again was the postseason.

Before that, there were several reasons for Red Sox enthusiasm, especially for fans interested in the future stars of the franchise. Pedroia had been hitting consistently all season and would be the American League Rookie of the Year. Jonathan Papelbon was one of the best closers in baseball. Josh Beckett made the year-one to year-two adjustment with AL hitters, and that was enough for him to dominate them all season. A young man that I called *El Flaco* (the Skinny Man), Clay Buchholz, threw a no-hitter against the Orioles. Jacoby Ellsbury, the center fielder drafted in Johnny Damon's final Red Sox season, made his debut. He was phenomenal, so much so that he provided an immediate threat to Coco Crisp's job. And while Dice-K didn't reach Greg Maddux levels, he was pretty good as a rookie. I wasn't surprised that he didn't blow people away here like he did in Japan. This is major league baseball. I know there are some good players in Japan, but there's no way the variety of pitchers and hitters there is equal to what we have in the majors.

I wasn't much for talking about the future when there were championships to be won right then and there, but I started to understand some things better after playing, listening, and watching during the 2007 season. I had new insight into why Theo was so protective of his territory in baseball operations. These kids he'd drafted or signed were all fun players to watch. I couldn't imagine scouting and developing all this talent and then being told what you could or couldn't do with it. I also got a better grasp of why the fans were so excited about the future. The kids slid right into the team culture, so it was natural to project what they were going to be when they matured as players, and how long they'd be staying in Boston.

Personally, I felt that everything I cared about was coming together and fitting together. On the field, I didn't think any pitcher was capable of fooling me for long. I'd lock myself in a room studying video if I had to figure out what the approach was against me. Once I got it, I relied on my memory and instincts to handle everything else. Although I didn't hit as many home runs as the previous season, I was a better hitter. My average rose to a career high .332, I was on base 44 percent of the time, and I slugged at a .621 percentage.

I felt confident about what I was doing, and I didn't mind sharing what I knew. If I had a friend on another team and I could see him having problems with his swing or something, I'd tell him. This is a hard game. If I could help out a friend, I'd do it. Another way I shared was through a book. A Boston sportswriter, Tony Massarotti, asked me in 2006 if I wanted to tell my story. I'd told him yes because I knew my story and it was a positive one. I'd overcome a lot to get where I was, and I wanted to pass that information on to someone who might need inspiration. That book was published in 2007 by St. Martin's Press.

My popularity began to reach levels that required a new routine with my agents of sorting through endorsement offers, business-partnership proposals, and requests to make appearances. I appreciated the love, but there had been something normal about the days when I'd pull up to the Lenox Hotel in Boston, begin to park my car there, and then be instructed by one of the valets, "I'm sorry, sir, you can't leave your car here. You'll have to go somewhere else." Back then, it would take another valet to say, "Hey, I think that's David

Ortiz. He can stay." It was fine to be recognized by some and not others. I used to walk down Boylston Street all the time, strolling along without ever being stopped.

Those days were over. It was time for Tiffany and me to start thinking about moving again. We wanted to be in a community where we weren't isolated from people. We wanted our kids to go to public schools and have solid relationships with their friends, just like anyone else their age. Yet we also wanted to have the type of privacy where, if we decided to go outside, there wouldn't be a car stopping to point or people coming up to ring the doorbell. Overall, these were not problems. Not at all. They were just considerations we had to take more seriously than we ever had in the past.

I had no idea that the postseason was going to push my popularity — and the team's — to 2004 levels. We'd begun our 2004 playoff run by sweeping the Angels, and we did the same thing in 2007. Manny was back in the lineup, and I felt the difference instantly. It puts managers, pitching coaches, and pitchers in an uncomfortable position when they're dealing with a combo like Manny and me. In the Angels series, I had eight at-bats in three games with six walks and two home runs. My homers came in Games 1 and 3. Manny's eight at-bats produced five walks and two more home runs. He homered in Game 2 for a walk-off winner, and again in the third game to leave a mark in the series.

We were on to the league championship series to play the Indians. We needed every bit of our experience and luck and the contributions of every coach and player on the roster in this series. I say that because four games into the series, we were in trouble. We were down three games to one, with Beckett on the mound to save us in Game 5.

Beckett was a boss that night. The more he pitched, sharp and fearless, the more apparent it was that the loud Cleveland crowd wouldn't see their team clinching anything that night. Beckett had emerged as our ace in the regular season, winning 20 games, and he iced the biggest game of the whole year by giving up just a run while striking out 11.

Back at Fenway, there was still some nervousness about being eliminated in Game 6. That melted in the first inning when J. D. Drew came to the plate with the bases loaded. The fans hadn't been wild about J.D. all year. His numbers, across the board, were average. It may have burned him some whenever he struck out, but he'd never let the crowd see that side of him. What most people respected about him was his ability to draw a walk when necessary. That was a thought when he faced Fausto Carmona with two outs in the bottom of the first. Anything to push a run across.

Then it happened. I was on first base, so I saw everything.

On a 3-1 count, often a take pitch for J.D., Carmona threw a fastball right down the middle of the plate. I knew what Carmona was thinking. He needed a strike, he didn't want to walk in a run, and J.D. was a patient hitter. Maybe he thought J.D. would take that one too. But the pitch was too good to pass on. J.D. swung and drove it deep to center field. He hit it well, he knew it, and so did the Fenway crowd. He got his loudest ovation of the year when the long drive reached the camera well in center and officially became a grand slam. I had never seen J.D. so pumped, and it was good to see. I waited to greet him at the plate and yelled over the crowd, "That's what I'm talkin' about!" That's the playoffs summed up in that one at-bat. Sometimes you're struggling and no one is thinking about you, and in one swing of the bat you put yourself right back on the map.

We knew we were going to win the game right then. And I couldn't see any way where we'd lose a Game 7 at Fenway, with starting pitcher Dice-K on the mound. It was a great game, but it wasn't the game we expected. I knew we'd win the pennant, but I didn't think it would happen with a six-run eighth, on our way to an 11–2 win.

As for the World Series, when I ask Tiffany what she remembers from it, she talks about all our friends. I think that's the side of baseball that's most memorable. I obsessively prepared for all the games, and I gave everything I had to the game every season that I played. I remember all the big hits and spectacular plays. But I'm with Tiffany: it's the people moments, the relationships, that stay with you forever.

So do I remember playing the Colorado Rockies in the World Series and sweeping them? Without a doubt. I remember how Beckett, the ALCS MVP, pitched like an MVP in Game 1 of the Series. In a tighter Game 2, I remember Papelbon picking off Matt Holliday for the third out of the eighth in a 2–1 game. When we got to Denver, it was all about the kids again. Four hits at the top of the lineup for Ellsbury and three for Pedroia. The winning pitcher was Dice-K.

But this is what I mean by relationships. The winning pitcher in Game 4 was Jon Lester, who I'd prayed about at the end of 2006. Cancer. Who knew, in September 2006, if Lester had pitched his final game in the majors? He was the story of 2006 because he had gotten sick. He was the story of 2007 because he had not only fought cancer and overcome it, but come back to accomplish the hardest thing in the sport: winning your last game of the season so your team can win the final game of the season. Seeing him out there meant a lot to me. Like Pedroia, Lester was one of the young guys who had no sense of entitlement. He was a good listener, and I could see that he was modeling himself after Beckett. It was our established ace, Beckett, who began the Series and our future ace who ended it.

It was a blessing to be a part of that night and that team. I remember going back to our Denver hotel after the game and sitting in the lobby with representatives from all aspects of the team. The owners were there with their wives and kids. The coaches and players, the doctors and trainers. We were all there, and a team executive, Charles Steinberg, was playing the piano. He knew what he was doing with those keys. He'd finish one song and I'd want him to play another one. He had started with "Yesterday" and "And I Love Her" from the Beatles. It was an organizational sing-along at that point, and it went from the Beatles to Elton John to Billy Joel to James Taylor. I remember being surprised when Charles told me that he composed and played his own music as well. And then he played it. Time didn't matter at that point. It was the Red Sox at our best, all of us singing, laughing, and swaying along.

I'll always remember those nights, bigger than baseball nights.

12

Another Country

It was a warm summer morning at Columbia Point, and I'd arrived early for my appointment at the John F. Kennedy Library. The extra time, and the occasion, inspired me to look out at Dorchester Bay, pause, and reflect on some pivotal moments in my life.

As I prepared for a private lunch in my honor, I recalled the highs and lows of my childhood: my parents making dozens of sacrifices so we could have more food and perhaps one day move to a better house and attend better schools; my dad always fixing someone else's car while often not having a car of his own to drive; my mom leaving the Dominican to buy clothes, dolls, and fabrics in places like Curaçao to bring back home and sell to tourists. My dad would take her to the airport on one of the vehicles we had, either his motorcycle or her moped. I could still remember them motoring away, two people and a suitcase. In those days, I didn't see my father much outside of Sundays because he was always doing a job to get extra money.

This day, June 11, 2008, was right in front of me. This was the day I would officially become a United States citizen. The ceremony was supposed to be about the present, and that's why I had a reserved seat in the front row, one of 226 people who would be granted American citizenship this day. It promised to be a great day, a day when some would say that they'd become U.S. citizens at the same time as Big Papi. But for me, the day wasn't solely about the achievements of Papi. That was the pleasant part of the story, the part where the baseball star wins in the end with a clutch hit. That wasn't the whole story, though. The past had also made this day significant, so I continued my slow memory walk through that part of the story. And I did it with gratitude.

I remembered moving to a new house in the Dominican after my parents had separated, though my dad was still a big part of my life. I'd come home from school with a friend, and my dad would look him up and down before giving a verdict. If he didn't get a good feeling, if he didn't like what he saw, he'd say, "David, you're not going to be his friend anymore." And that would be it. If my mother and father told me what I was supposed to do, I'd do it. No questions asked.

It was perfect that, all these years later, my father was at the JFK Library for the lunch and ceremony. He was the one who searched for any fear or indecision in my teenage voice when I called him after my first few weeks in the United States. He never told me that he and the family were counting on me, but I knew that they were. And I could hear that in *his* voice. He wanted to be assured that I'd stay the course and find a way to make a career out of pro baseball. I was driven by his hope and guided by the wisdom he'd given me through the years.

The adversity along the way had made me stronger. It made the adversity I'd experienced two weeks earlier, hurting my left wrist in a game against the Orioles, seem trivial. At least my father and my family didn't have to work as hard as they had back then. At least my children, twelve, seven, and three years old, didn't have to face any of the conditions in their neighborhood that I had in mine.

I was so proud to stand there and bring our family closer together.

I never dreamed of this when I met Tiffany Brick from Kaukauna, Wisconsin, in 1996. I didn't have my eye on citizenship then, but I always took the rules of the country seriously. Once, in the minors, there was a wild fight in a nightclub between my teammates and some of the Wisconsin locals. It was mayhem, and I was angry at the way my boys had been treated. I remember peeling teammates from the fray, trying to keep them out of trouble. Tiffany said to me later, "You were mad, and those guys were being real assholes to you and your teammates. I'm surprised you didn't knock them out." I told her, simply, "I'm a big guy and I can really hurt someone, and I don't want to do that." She would tell that story every now and then, and she'd add that she was impressed that someone at 20 years old could consistently think before acting. I gave credit to my parents then, and continue to give them credit now. They never let their circumstances define who they were. They demanded respect and high character.

Thank God that my youth, my ego, my testosterone never got the best of me. I'm fortunate that I've never gotten a speeding ticket in the United States. No arrests. No time in jail. The country has been incredible for me and my family, and I've always wanted to show that I respect the boundaries that are in place.

On June 11, I got emotional as I stood there with the others reciting the Pledge of Allegiance. I thought of what is said in the Pledge, and even what isn't said. That's the part that got me. As a new citizen, I felt as though the country was saying, "We trust you." I was so appreciative. I brought my family in for a hug and held on tight. I knew I'd be spending a lot of time with them that day, and that later they'd be there watching the game.

The wrist injury hadn't gotten any better. What had happened Memorial Day weekend was that the sheath covering the tendons in my left wrist had been dislodged on a hard swing. My pain threshold is high, but this wasn't just about pain, it was also about the mechanics of my wrist. It just didn't feel right. After reaching a full count, the damaged wrist felt so awkward that I had to come out of the game.

I had no guesses on what it was. I knew it was bad, though. My wrist felt terrible. Things got even more frustrating when I talked with the doctors and was told about the healing and treatment plan for the wrist. There would be no surgery or resetting. I was just going to have to wear a cast and be patient. "Is that it?" I'd asked. "Nothing else?"

That was it, and it was nerve-racking.

I'd begun the season slowly, hitting just .184 in April. I was starting to get hot in May. I hit eight home runs and eight doubles, drew 18 walks, and drove in 22 runs. Not a bad month at all. We were playing good baseball, but there was a twist to the season that we weren't used to. We had company. It wasn't just the Red Sox and Yankees anymore. The team that had spent nearly a decade at the bottom of the division, the Tampa Bay Rays, was challenging for the East title. We needed all the slugging I could give us, and I was starting to do that. But at the precise moment when my team needed me, I could only observe.

That seemed like the story of what the season would be for the Red Sox. Some things were damaged far beyond repair, and we could only watch them play out. I knew at least a month before everyone else that Manny had reached a breaking point with the Red Sox. There was no way the relationship could last any longer. It was hard for me to watch because of who Manny was to me and how I felt about winning games.

I just couldn't crush Manny like some people did. He was only four years older than me, but I looked up to him as a hitter. He was a genius at the plate. All you have to do is ask the pitchers. They'll tell you that he could be fooled, like all of us, but he couldn't be fooled for long. He studied a pitcher's strengths and then worked until that strength wasn't as reliable for the pitcher as it had been in the past. I loved that about him.

The other stuff was tough. I wanted to win every night, and when he was there, winning was more likely. Now flip that around: when he wasn't there, it made it a lot harder for us to be successful. Manny would change his mind like day changing to night. He had spent the beginning of spring training saying that he wanted the Red Sox to pick up the option years on his contract and he wanted to finish his career in Boston. He joked and smiled a lot. Then, right before I got hurt, he started to change. It was clear to me that he was sick of New England, more fed up than he'd ever been, and wanted to get out. Over the years, Tito had called meetings with a few veterans to talk about Manny, and he'd tell us that he could easily take Manny out of the lineup. But he warned us that we would have to be okay with how that would look on the field. Most of the time, we agreed to put some humor on his actions and keep it moving.

But I knew Manny, and this was different. He wasn't giving anyone a choice.

On opening night of the NBA Finals between the Celtics and Lakers, the Red Sox moved first pitch of our game with Tampa up an hour so we wouldn't have a conflict with the Celtics. Instead, it turned out that we had a conflict with ourselves. Everyone was aware of how intense Kevin Youkilis, our first baseman, could be when he played. He was known for throwing anything in sight when things didn't go his way during an at-bat. Even before there was any trouble with Youkilis, Manny would tell me, "If he ever hits me with a helmet or anything, I'm going to have to hit him back."

Youkilis didn't hit Manny with a stray bat, helmet, or anything else in the fifth inning that night against Tampa. But Manny slapped at him anyway, and they had to be separated in the dugout. Nothing like that had ever happened with Manny before, but it faded quickly over the next couple of weeks. The city was entertained and distracted by other things. The Celtics won the Finals and had a parade, just eight months after we had celebrated winning the World Series over the Rockies. And we were back in first place, even without me in the middle of the lineup.

The end, unofficially, came on a Friday night in Houston. I don't think Manny did it on purpose, but once it happened he understood that there was no coming back from it. He'd asked Jack McCormick, our traveling secretary, who had been with the Red Sox for a dozen years, to find 16 tickets for that night's game. Jack didn't think he'd be able to find that many, and an argument broke out. Then Jack was on the floor, put there by a Manny push. It didn't go any further than that, but that was far enough.

We won that night's game in Houston, and then dropped five in a row. Three of those losses were to Tampa, which regained control of first place and went ahead by three and a half games. We were sliding. We were five games back after a one-run loss at Yankee Stadium on July 6. Manny pinch-hit that day in the ninth inning against Mariano Rivera. I knew, because he'd gotten me many times, how masterful Mariano could be. When he faced Manny with the score tied at 4 in the ninth, he needed three pitches to get him out. Three called strikes. Manny never moved his bat. We lost the game in the bottom of the 10th.

A lot of reporters and fans wondered if that strikeout was intentional. Did Manny really stand there to send a message to ownership and the front office? No one really knew. The fact that the question had to be asked was a sign that we were slipping, and it had nothing to do with the standings. We were too talented a team to miss the playoffs. But there was tension in the clubhouse. I wanted to get back in the lineup as fast as I could, and that would help some. Manny being granted his wish would also be healthy for everyone.

The trading deadline was approaching, and my wrist was healed.

But it just didn't feel like it belonged to me. The first time I started taking swings, I remember thinking, *I have no chance*. I'm telling you, it was bad. I was getting a lot of massages and doing various wrist exercises. It was going to be a while before I felt like myself.

It must have been an eye-opening time for Red Sox ownership and management. It was nearly August, the stretch run, and for different reasons they weren't seeing the real David Ortiz and the real Manny Ramírez. Manny seemed to be making a deadline push to get what he wanted. He talked on his phone, during a game, by the Green Monster. Another time he said he was hurt. In yet another incident, he made himself available to reporters, in English and Spanish, and told them that he was sick of the Red Sox. He even said that "the Red Sox don't deserve a player like me."

All of this happened in a three-week span, and then he was gone. On July 31, the Red Sox, Pirates, and Dodgers pulled off a three-team deal. We got Jason Bay. The Dodgers got Manny Ramírez. It was the best thing for everyone, even if it didn't seem that way on the surface. Bay was a good player and teammate. Manny was a Hall of Famer. But he was a Hall of Famer who wanted to leave, and so it was clear that no one would see his true talent until he got what he wanted.

I didn't know what to think, short- and long-term. We needed to make the playoffs, and after I'd missed all of June and nearly all of July, I didn't think my bat could carry us. And Manny was gone. That was the bad news. The good news was that Youkilis and Pedroia were having MVP-type seasons. Pedroia, in just his second year, was one of the respected leaders in the clubhouse. If I'd had an MVP vote, he would have been my choice.

I tried not to think about how good we'd have been if we, not the Dodgers, could have had the focused Manny. Manny went to L.A. and destroyed National League pitching. His numbers were ridiculous. They were so ridiculous that it didn't take long for him to be mentioned as a MVP candidate in the NL.

This was my sixth year in Boston, and our team had been serious contenders for all six of those seasons. There were so many accomplished players I'd been able to call a teammate. Nomar. Pedro. Johnny. Manny. Some of the best players the game had ever seen, and then they were gone. It was never pleasant on the way out. Contract breakdowns. Cheap shots from the media. Hard feelings between players and the organization.

Why was that? And was it going to happen to me?

It was hard for me to envision that at the end of the 2008 season. I'd always wanted my contracts to have more money in them, and the Red Sox always wanted it to be less. That was the nature of business. It wasn't personal. As for the media, I understood what their job was. Most of the time the media had been fair and respectful to me, so I didn't have any problems there. Our team, even without Manny, didn't give people much reason to complain.

We lost the division to Tampa, but we still made the playoffs for the fifth time in the previous six seasons. In what was becoming an annual October series, we played the Angels in the first round. For the third time in five years, we eliminated them. Winning that round earned us a spot in the league championship series against Tampa.

I had a lot of respect for that team. Their lineup never scared you, but their pitching was unbelievable. Their manager, Joe Maddon, was one of the first managers to use a defensive shift against me. He used to come up with some crazy shit. At times, honestly, his alignments would frustrate me and get me out of my game plan. One time he put on a shift and I got a mistake pitch. I hit it out and thought, *You're gonna have to put a shift in the stands to get that one*. He was a great manager, and his team really played hard for him.

I was playing hard in the postseason, but my swing was off. I had more walks than hits, and my slugging percentage was in the .300s. The Rays played a solid, and unpredictable, series. We beat them in Game 1, but they won the next three in a row. After outscoring us 31–13, they did it to us again in Game 5 at Fenway and were winning 7–0 after seven innings. TBS was televising the series, and friends of mine told me that the network was doing a Rays-Phillies World Series preview during the game. I know I looked bad, and so did the team.

But we were a veteran team with a lot of talent and pride. We made it a game in the bottom of the seventh. It was 7–1 when I came to the plate, with two guys on. One thing that amazes visiting teams about Fenway is that the fans never, ever think that we're out of a game. The comeback in 2004 has a lot to do with that, but I remember that hopefulness from 2003 too. As I walked up, I could hear the sellout crowd chanting my name. *Papi, Papi, Papi.* I was facing a hard-throwing reliever named Grant Balfour, who usually had nasty stuff. He was scuffling a bit in Game 5, and although he was still throwing in the upper 90s, his pitches weren't moving all that much.

As I look back at that swing now, I can see what I couldn't then: the swing had a big loop in it. At least it's big to my eye. I was compensating for the awkwardness in my wrist, and it was going to take a while for me to figure that out. It didn't matter when Balfour threw a 97-mile-per-hour fastball right where I like it, low and inside. I pulled it to right field, and the three-run shot put us right back in the game and the series.

We won Games 5 and 6, which put us in Tampa for Game 7. Their starter was Matt Garza, who pitched well against us. Ours was Jon Lester. A year after his cancer treatment, Lester was much bigger and stronger than he had been the previous October in Denver. His mentality reminded me of my own. He was the kind of athlete who wanted to wipe out everybody in front of him. He was always ready for competition, never scared.

Lester threw hard and had great control all night. We didn't give him much to work with, though, coming up with just three hits. Not only did the Rays win the pennant with a 3–1 win, they gave a glimpse of their future in the eighth and ninth innings. They brought out a left-hander named David Price to finish the game. He'd been the number-one overall pick in the draft the year before, and he was already in the majors. He was 23, and the bullpen assignment was temporary. He was going to be a star, and we'd have to deal with him at the top of their rotation for many years.

If Tampa's future looked good, so did ours. I liked the youth we had, and unlike Tampa, we had the ability to spend to fill some of our holes. I had obviously been happier, as a baseball player, in October 2007 than I was in October 2008. My life, though, was never supposed to be about baseball and nothing else.

After taking a year off to better plan the Children's Fund, I removed a couple of training wheels and we became a 501(c)(3) in 2008. We got a board of directors. We also put on our first celebrity golf classic in the Dominican. My friend and teammate Sean Casey was our emcee. It was attended by some of the biggest names in sports, past and present: Bobby Orr, John Havlicek, Mariano Rivera, Luis Tiant, Jimmy Rollins, Torii Hunter, Jim Rice.

I was humbled and optimistic. These great athletes had taken the time to come to Punta Cana to support something that was so important to me. I enjoyed the beautiful Dominican weather with them, the golf, the food, and their conversations and smiles. We'd done all that while raising money to help those who truly needed it. It was hard to grasp that this was happening to me. Just over 100 miles down the road from Punta Cana, not that long ago, I had been one of those poor kids, never thinking that Hall of Famers would be coming to the Dominican for me.

It was a fulfilling time in my life, and as a positive thinker, I had no reason to believe that it would soon become a nightmare. I absolutely did not think like that. But the nightmare happened anyway.

13

Accused

As I sat at ease in Fort Myers before a crowd of reporters, it never occurred to me that this session would one day be used as proof of my hypocrisy.

Why would it? It was February 16, 2009, my first interview of spring training. I'd done this for years. This was part of the routine. The men and women who cover and comment on the Red Sox would ask me questions about numerous topics, and I'd give them answers. Simple, for them and for me.

The sun was usually brilliant, the mood mostly light, and the questions the friendliest they'd be all year. *How was the off-season? What did you work on? What do you think of the team this year?* When it was over, there'd still be time for golf, sailing, or the beach.

I never think that someone is trying to be an asshole, and I didn't think that way that day when I was asked about steroid use in baseball. I understood the timing of the question. A week earlier, Alex Rodriguez of the Yankees had admitted to using performance-enhancing drugs (PEDs) for parts of two years, from 2001 until 2003. He said he did it while he played in Texas, it was stupid to do, and he hadn't done any of that during his five seasons in New York.

It was a hot topic, and it had gone beyond baseball. Even President Obama chimed in with his opinion, when asked. It was national news.

I was asked what I would do, in today's game, if someone tested positive for PEDs. I was happy to answer the question. I hated how some people talked about baseball, especially when a player was doing something special. There was always that suggestion of steroids, and I thought it was unfair to the player and the game. I told the reporters that I would never use PEDs because it would be disrespectful to a lot of people, including my family and the fans. I said there should be testing three or four times a year, for everyone, and that if someone failed a drug test, they should be banned for an entire season.

I wasn't trying to embarrass anyone, even if most Red Sox fans wouldn't have minded a takedown of Alex. I wasn't afraid to say that I liked Alex and considered him a friend. Some of the people hanging around him wanted something from him, whether it was money or fame, but all I ask of anyone is to be themselves. I think that's why I get along with so many different personality types. I'm not asking you to be who I want you to be. Just be yourself, and that's good enough.

That's how I viewed that February exchange with the reporters. I was being myself, speaking out about a subject on which I had some passionate opinions. I didn't like how Latin players were routinely accused of using PEDs. Although no one went there with me, they'd tiptoe up to that line and not cross it. They'd ask, essentially, why are you so good now and you weren't in Minnesota? I'd usually give a polite answer, although I wasn't the one who should have been answering. It was obvious that the difference in my performance there was more of a Twins problem than my problem. I was a part-time player my last year in Minnesota, and I had a .500 slugging percentage. I had 32 doubles and 20 home runs. As a part-timer. How many more would I have hit as a full-time player? How many more would I have hit as a full-time player who didn't have a manager fucking with his head year after year? Ten? Fifteen? And that was based purely on the talent of a 27-year-old hitter, not the proven ability of the studying, thinking slugger I'd become in Boston.

After making my statements in Florida, I didn't give any more thought to the state of major league baseball's drug policies. In 2003, players had been given a survey drug test, the results of which would remain anonymous. If at least 5 percent of players showed positive results, we would have mandatory testing, with penalties, in 2004.

We got the testing in 2004. I was fine with it. I've always been a big man, with raw, natural strength. I was that way even when I was just 15 or 16. When I became a pro, I used training supplements and vitamins, just like anyone else in baseball, to prepare for the season. Once the policy was put in place, teams were very specific about what would and would not trigger a positive test, and anyone who cared about his livelihood listened carefully.

That wasn't my concern at the beginning of the 2009 season. My left wrist was. Still. I had gotten into some bad habits from the previous year's injury, and they carried over into the season. My swing was wrecked, and I was connecting under the ball all the time, under, under, under . . . I couldn't get on top of it. Nobody worried in April. We had an 11-game winning streak, and the fact that I didn't have a home run in the month could be explained as a slow start.

It got more serious in May. I was struggling, badly, and I was in the middle of two extremes. On one side were the media and fans, many of whom decided I was done. Washed up at 33 years old. The other side was my team. You wouldn't think there's a downside to always being reliable, game after game, year after year. There is. Sometimes your organization looks at you like you're Superman. I was such a good hitter that people couldn't understand why I was going through such a nasty slump. Even when people tried to say something to me, they didn't know what to tell me.

Thirty games into the season, I still hadn't homered. I had a .220

batting average. I was in the same city I'd been since 2003, parking in the same Fenway lot, walking through the same clubhouse. But now, for the first time, I personally experienced the cynical New England that I'd heard about. All the superstar Red Sox players had dealt with it, for one reason or another, over the years. No exceptions. Now it was my turn. I don't know if they thought they were going to wear me down, or get me to snap, but they had no chance. I thought of that warning from Manny. *Don't ever change the menu in Boston . . .*

But suddenly it was controversial to bring up Manny in Boston. On May 8, the news broke that he had tested positive for a banned substance that masks PED use. He was suspended for 50 games. For some, it brought into question all that he — and by association, we — had accomplished. The trend for players with Hall of Fame talent and PED suspensions was that they had no chance of being voted into the Hall. The writers with votes weren't just guardians, they were embarrassed guardians. The steroid era had been going on for years without anyone writing and talking about it. When it was clear that several voters were late to the conversation, many of them became zealots on PEDs. It was as if they were determined to never miss a story like that again.

For me, two things can be simultaneously true without contradiction: Manny used a drug to mask a PED, *and* he was still one of the best hitters I'd ever seen.

The niceties were gone now with the Manny news. The innuendo was part of the new story. He's Dominican and so am I. We were teammates. I described him as an idol of mine. If he did it, then it was assumed I did too. Or so the logic went. I knew I didn't have to answer for anything. My career had exploded because I learned how to work hard, study, and claim my place as a middle-of-the-order hitter.

I knew how to listen too.

A friend of mine from the Dominican had called me after I'd hit my first home run, on May 20, our team's 40th game of the year. He's known me since we were kids, and we'd played together on traveling teams.

"Papi," he said. "You're too loopy!"

I asked him what he was talking about.

"Your bottom hand is taking over every swing," he said. "That's why you're missing so many pitches. It's why you're popping up so many pitches."

He made so much sense. My body naturally wanted to protect the left wrist. I hadn't been using my body the way I normally would.

"Go and have fun, man," my friend said. "What's the worst thing that can happen? Oh-for-four? Who cares? Enjoy yourself."

I started doing hand-strengthening exercises. The fact that it felt so uncomfortable told me that I hadn't been using my top hand. I did them for about a week, and then I started feeling it.

I took my friend's advice, as awkward as the wrist felt, and forced myself to focus on the range of motion in my left hand. Whereas I had one home run in the first two months of the season, I piled up 12 in the next two months.

That's where I stood on a Thursday morning at the end of July, a morning that I'll never forget. It was July 30. I was standing in our ancient clubhouse, the same one that Babe Ruth and Ted Williams used in an earlier era. I felt like I had seen them, or some type of ghost, after a reporter I didn't know approached. He told me something I thought was a joke, a truly unfunny one.

"Any minute, you're going to see your name flash on ESPN," he said. "You tested positive for a banned substance in 2003, and your name is on The List."

The reporter was youngish and had thick dark hair. He was Michael Schmidt of the *New York Times,* and he was one of the star reporters on the PED beat. Someone had told him that my name, and Manny's, appeared on a supposedly anonymous list of 104 players from the survey test of 2003. The list had been seized by the federal government, and now had become a bit of a political weapon. No one knew who was doing the leaking and whom or what they were fighting against.

The real story was complicated and needed to be walked through slowly. That list didn't mean what everyone thought it did. Some people on it were steroid users, some were supplement users, some were amphetamine users, and some used something over-the-counter that activated a positive test. They were all lumped in there. But the topic was sexy enough that I knew it wasn't going to head in the direction of reasoned analysis. It was a PEDs story, and it followed an admission from Alex and a fall by Manny. I was having a below-average season that had caused people to ask whether I had been doing something previously and perhaps stopped doing it in 2009.

It all added up to cheating and nothing else for a lot of people.

I was now a name in this war. It was endless. Say you didn't do it enough and you sound guilty. Say nothing and your silence proves your guilt. Your spoken truth can't get you out of it because the assumption is that you're lying if you say you didn't do it. Everybody lies about it, right? Even your advocates can't get you out of it. They mean well, but their position is often built on guilt. *It wasn't illegal at the time,* they say. Or, *I don't care what they do; it's entertainment.*

But that wasn't how I saw it. I didn't do it. I did care. In fact, I gave a damn. It was my career, my name, my reputation. Who was going to believe that I hated the thought of chemicals in my body and I had never used steroids? As a professional athlete, I'd trained hard and used vitamins and supplements like anyone else. I was careful about what I put in my body in 2003. I became even more conscientious in 2004, when Major League Baseball issued specific guidelines about what could and could not be used. I'd never failed a drug test in the five years the policy had been in place, and never worried about failing because I wasn't doing anything wrong. Who was going to trust what I'd had to say after that relaxed session in spring training, even though every word of it had been true?

I said before that it was a nightmare. It was worse than that. It was a horror movie.

It took me a while to calm down, because I had so much shit going through my head. Did this guy know what he was talking about? I needed to call my agent. The union. My wife. And we had a game to play that afternoon, followed by trips to Baltimore, Tampa, and New York.

I hit a home run on the 30th, and we beat the A's. I remember a lot of my homers, but not that one. There was plenty to learn, and I needed to understand and retain it all by the time we got to New York. That's where I wanted to handle all the questions. I'd planned to go to Yankee Stadium, in the largest media center in the country, and show everyone that I wasn't hiding. I was going to speak for myself, in English, without notes, and the people would see my honesty and consistency.

At the time, I just didn't know better. I was too optimistic. I thought if I shared everything I knew with the public, maybe all fans, not just Red Sox fans, would be able to see my point of view. In an unusual move, Major League Baseball released a statement, putting its support behind me. Michael Weiner, the head of the Players' Association, was a frequent visitor to my suite in the Marriott Marquis in New York. I wanted to be sure I knew everything that he did, so that when I talked I'd be informed.

In some cities—even in Boston—it was too late. The opinions had already been firmly set.

"Big Papi was on the juice," Bob Ryan wrote in the *Boston Globe,* "and only the terminally naive could be shocked."

"David Ortiz lied to you," the *Globe*'s Dan Shaughnessy added. "It seems safe to say that his entire Red Sox career is a lie."

Believe it or not, even the cowriter of my first book, Tony Massarotti, called me a myth.

Inside our clubhouse, guys supported me, even if they didn't know what to say. Or what to think.

I couldn't blame a soul in the organization. They honestly didn't know what to do, and I understood that because I didn't either. I was confused, angry, and alone. I was being accused in 2009 for something that happened in 2003 and no one could tell me what I did. I thought it was bullshit. It had been the early stages of testing, and part of the experiment was to record names, but with an assurance they'd be kept confidential. I had a feeling back then that this type of privacy breach would happen to somebody. Just not me.

What I couldn't accept was the combination of snap judgments and lack of information being brought to my own case.

"Hey, Papi, you tested positive for something."

"Oh yeah? What was it?"

"We don't know. We just know it's positive."

How does that make sense? To me, it didn't and doesn't. Because of "The List," the Red Sox couldn't say they were all the way riding with me, because they didn't know what I'd done. Theo Epstein didn't know. Terry Francona didn't know. My teammates and the Players' Association didn't know.

I knew it would stay that way until I was proven right or someone proved that I was wrong.

Think about it: the first test for PEDs was in 2003, and PED use started to be punished in 2004. I had done my best work in the testing era, not the steroid era.

I don't know how many players looked forward to being questioned by the national media, inside Yankee Stadium, but I did. It had been a week and a half since the *Times* story was published, and it was all I'd thought about during that time. I was in a hurry to learn what had happened to me, and in a hurry to share it with the public.

My press conference was scheduled on a Saturday, although our four-game series with the Yankees began on a Thursday. If I wanted a preview of how the typical fan was going to receive my explanation, it was there in the series opener. I stepped to the plate for my first at-bat, and instead of the usual murmur, a mixture of respect and envy, there was something different coming from the crowd of nearly 50,000. Boos. Loud, pointed, disappointed boos. It wasn't the whole crowd, but their displeasure was the most pronounced sound of the night.

This was going to be my reality until I spoke about why I was on that list. I also acknowledged that it might be my reality even after I spoke.

My moment came that Saturday afternoon, inside a packed room at the stadium. There were dozens of reporters there from New York, Boston, Los Angeles, Chicago. I kept telling myself that I had no reason to be nervous because I was just telling my story. Weiner sat next to me so he could answer the questions that dealt with legalities and technicalities. That wasn't my area. I was there to answer the big questions: What happened? What did you do? I patiently told the media what I thought went wrong.

I said, "I definitely was a little bit careless back in those days when I was buying supplements and vitamins over the counter. Legal supplements, legal vitamins, over-the-counter. But I never bought steroids or used steroids."

It was the truth. And after I said it, I felt some of the tension leave my body. All I could share was the truth. It was up to them, and the fans, whether they wanted to believe it. There were many questions from the crowd, regarding what I took and why it had triggered the positive test. One person asked if I wanted to see the anonymous list released so all the names would be known to the public. The idea be-ing that I wouldn't be the only player fighting for his reputation. But I've always been a positive person, so why would I root for making someone else miserable just because I was going through some shit? That's incredibly selfish. This is how I answered the reporter:

"I don't think that I would really like to see another player going through what I've been through this past week."

After I spoke in New York, I could see where my season and my story were headed. It wasn't to the depths, as many might have imagined. We were playing in Texas about a week after I'd spoken from the heart in New York, and Tiffany and the kids came along. I was on the field, so I didn't hear about an incident that happened until the game was over. There was a guy yelling "Cheater" at me during each of my at-bats. D'Angelo was five years old, and he was hurt by what he heard.

I sat down with my son, who was a month away from going to kindergarten. I tried to tell him what the name-calling and jeers from the crowd meant. It needed to be explained, and I wanted to be the one who did it. But it killed me. I could see that he was confused, and he didn't understand what I was trying to tell him. At the end of our chat, I told him that you can't make everyone happy. I told him that on the playground there might be a kid who gets the attention because he screams louder than everyone else. On my playground, there are those who use microphones and I don't. They get the last word when it comes to telling the story and influencing the fans that way.

But that was just talking.

In 2009, my average didn't rise much, and I finished at .238. I did have 28 home runs and 99 runs batted in, which prompted one of my new teammates, Víctor Martínez, to joke, "They say this is a bad season for you? Close to thirty and a hundred? I wanna have bad seasons like this."

I'd learned a lot from my struggles at the plate, from the accusations made against me, and from being exposed to the dark side of the Boston media. It all required a fight, and I was ready. I'm a fighter and a winner. I learned to do both, to fight and to win, as a kid. You can knock me down, but I'm gonna get back up, brother. I'm gonna get back up.

14

Written Off

The author of a *Boston Globe* article had the right idea, but it didn't play out the way the story predicted. Or even the way I thought it would. The piece was written the day after the news broke about my name being on the 2003 list of performance-enhancing drug users in baseball. The reporter talked to multiple experts who said that advertisers would run away from me now, because who wanted to be connected to an accused cheater?

The story said that my "reign as the face of the Red Sox has probably come to an end as companies seek to distance themselves from the scandal."

I was associated with several companies in the summer of 2009, including giants like JetBlue and Reebok. I honestly had no idea what they would do after hearing the bad news. They stayed with me in the first week of August, when I gave the press conference in New York City and explained that I was not a steroid user. They stood by eight weeks later in October, when we made the playoffs and, for the first time, were swept by the Angels. In December, many of my sponsors and friends were in the Dominican for the golf classic, which was bigger than ever, with more sponsors, more auction items, more celebrities.

Ultimately, the sponsors didn't run away, as the story suggested they would, and for that I was grateful. An easy counterargument, of course, is to say that they didn't run away because I was helping their bottom line. It's all about the money, right?

Then how does that explain the doubts about me, and the disrespect toward me, in the New England media? As a member of the Red Sox, the successful and entertaining Red Sox, I was helping the media make money too. That didn't stop them from talking trash and dismissing me. And even closer to home was my manager, Terry Francona. I think I helped put him on the map and put some money in his pocket. I was good for his business. But just a few weeks into the 2010 season, before our team had played 25 games and before I'd reached 100 at-bats, he wasn't by my side anymore. Even he had lost faith in my baseball abilities.

I was mad. Mad at my manager, mad at columnists who wanted me on the bench, mad at sports talk show hosts who wanted to run me out of town. Anyone who thought that I was just going to be pushed aside and told to go home because they thought it was time for it to happen, I had some words for. A lot of the words were in my head. They were the late-night motivation I needed for extra study. They were there with me in the car as I drove to work, in the weight room, in the batting cage. I'm always real, so I'll tell you how serious it got: I began to look and listen for the outside criticism. I wanted it. I knew I could turn the hostility into my fuel, and it was going to help me get back to the player I knew I still was.

Seven years had passed since I'd been underestimated in Boston. But that had happened in 2003 because the majority of people in New England hadn't seen what I could do. In 2010, there was no excuse. I was 34 years old, and even though my 2009 hadn't been great, it was still better production than you'd get from the average hitter in baseball.

When it came to the media, I didn't want them to kiss my ass. I just

One of the proudest moments of my life. As a United States citizen, I felt as if the country was telling me, "We trust you."
Michael Ivins / Boston Red Sox

In 1996, I introduced myself to Tiffany Brick with an unforgettable line. Today she is my wife, best friend, and number one supporter. We're enjoying ourselves here at an event for the David Ortiz Children's Fund.
Paul Marotta / Getty Images

I never took the talk seriously, but Alex Rodriguez really was close to being traded for Manny and being my teammate in 2004. Instead, Manny stayed in Boston and four years later A-Rod was on our side — in the All-Star Game — at old Yankee Stadium.
Bloomberg / Getty Images

Here I'm side by side with Tito, which was usually the case, literally and figuratively. But he lost confidence in me one night in Toronto, and our relationship was never the same afterward.
Icon Sports Wire / Getty Images

Baseball gave me the opportunity to do so many things that I love: laugh, win, celebrate.
Michael Ivins / Boston Red Sox / Getty Images

Less than a week after the bombings on Marathon Monday, I was speaking from my heart at Fenway Park. What I eventually said surprised a lot of people, and I even surprised myself.
Michael Ivins / Boston Red Sox

There was no question that our collective baseball joy was restored in 2013.
Michael Ivins / Boston Red Sox / Getty Images

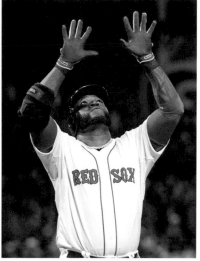

We knew that we could never fill the void that the tragedy had created in so many lives. The best thing we could do was honor the survivors, and the city, by embodying Boston Strong with our play.
Michael Ivins / Boston Red Sox / Getty Images

Every time I had a chance to honor my late mother, Angela, I did it.
Michael Ivins / Boston Red Sox / Getty Images

Our clubhouse desperately needed stability in 2013. John Farrell provided it in abundance the entire season. Michael Ivins/Boston Red Sox / Getty Images

I hit .688 in the World Series, but my wife said I was even better off the field as I put our family back together. That's why sharing this moment with my son, D'Angelo, was bigger than baseball.
Al Tielemans / Getty Images

For the first time in ninety-five years, the Red Sox clinched a World Series at Fenway. It was the most appropriate way to end a season that had begun so tragically.
Michael Ivins /
Boston Red Sox

I'd come such a long way. Initially, I was embarrassed by my Twins release. But times like these, collecting a necklace of championship rings, made me grateful for everything that had happened to me.
Michael Ivins / Boston Red Sox /
Getty Images

I remember what I was thinking when I first met Barack Obama: "As an American, you have to be proud to have a cool-ass president like this one."
Michael Ivins / Boston Red Sox

When I left the house for my final home opener, Tiffany said she didn't think the Red Sox had anything special planned. I should have known something was up. My daughter Alex brought me to tears with her beautiful singing of the National Anthem.
Michael Ivins /
Boston Red Sox / Getty Images

I'm always humbled to stand next to heroes such as Jeff Bauman, Marathon bombing survivor. His cooperation helped bring the perpetrators to justice.
Adam Glanzman /
Getty Images

I never considered myself just a baseball player. I had chances to make kids happy, to make all people happy, so I always tried to do that. Michael Ivins / Boston Red Sox / Getty Images

I continually felt the love from Fenway fans. I tried to give it back to them, with everything I had. Michael Ivins / Boston Red Sox / Getty Images

Many special guests attended my last regular-season game, but none more important than my father, Enrique. He's the hardest worker I know, and he saw a life for me in baseball long before I saw it for myself. Michael Ivins / Boston Red Sox / Getty Images

Pedro and Manny changed the way I thought about my job. More than that, their families and ours created a bond that continues to this day. Michael Ivins / Boston Red Sox / Getty Images

Reporters asked me if I had given my retirement speech any thought before this game, my last one at Fenway. I told them no. I thought our last game would come much later than it did.
Maddie Meyer / Getty Images

The fans of New England gave me their passion, and I tried to give it right back to them. Every game and every at-bat. They helped shape me as a player and as a man. Maddie Meyer / Getty Images

wanted them to use their heads. Just think about the order of things: in 2008, I'd injured the wrist on my top hand, and in 2009, for a few months, I couldn't hit for shit. I never heard anyone say, "Hey, it might have to do with the injury that he had the year before." Nope. It was just like, "He's old. He stinks. He can't hit no more. He can't do this, he can't do that . . ." Buried, buried, buried. Nobody talked about mechanics. Nobody talked about anything. Everything was based on, "He can't do it no more."

I believe the Boston media is powerful when it comes to the fans and, in some ways, influential when it comes to the way the team is managed. When the media make a big deal about something, when they create a problem or issue, what are the fans supposed to think? They figure that these people are around the team 24/7, so they must know what they're talking about. But they don't. As I said, their negativity was going to help me, but that's not the case for every player. Not every player wants a motherfucker in his face every single day, asking why he's struggling. I can put up with the pressure and the doubt because that's been my whole life, but some players don't want the hassle of Boston when the game itself is hard enough.

If all I'd had to do was prove the outsiders wrong, I would have had a smooth season. It wouldn't have mattered how much reporters tried to pit me against my teammate Mike Lowell. Mikey was my boy, a great third baseman, and MVP of the World Series in 2007. He hurt his right hip in 2008 and had to have surgery in the offseason. In 2009, he hit 17 home runs. By 2010, according to the media, we were similar players—at the end of our careers. Mikey had handled left-handed pitching well the previous year, hitting .301. I'd struggled, with a .212 average. The solution that started to gain a lot of popularity in the media was to turn us into a designated hitter platoon. He'd play against the lefties, and I'd have the righties. The television network owned by the team, NESN, even ran a poll about what should happen next.

I could have dealt with it all if that had been the extent of it. It wasn't. And I had no warning, not even a hint, of what was going to happen next.

Some events are so meaningful that every detail sticks. The sounds. The looks on individual faces in the crowd. The location of the cameras. Your teammates and their voices, voices that sound like a shouted echo when they're trying to get your attention. The awareness that everybody is looking in your direction, waiting to see how you'll react to the situation. The isolation. The anger. The disloyalty.

That was my night on April 27, 2010.

After a rough start to the season, we were looking more like the team we were expected to be. Our record, going into a Tuesday night game in Toronto, was 9-11. Twenty games into the season doesn't tell you much of anything. Lots of teams and players have hot starts, but so what? There's still 90 percent of the season to play, so the skill is in being able to maintain what you've started. The same is true for slow starts. If you have talent, you're going to work your way into a rhythm and get your timing down. That's the way I had always approached it, and I felt that it worked for me.

We were locked in a tight game with the Blue Jays, tied at 1 in the top of the eighth inning. I had made my name in moments like this. This was the part of the game — being presented with drama and an opportunity to win it — where I had the most fun. I was batting sixth in the lineup that night, one spot behind J. D. Drew. J.D. was good at recognizing pitches, so I knew there was a chance he'd get on base with two outs, which would load the bases for me.

I started thinking about who was in the Toronto bullpen and what kind of stuff they had. There was no question in my mind that I was going to be able to do something to help us get a win. I was in deep concentration on what was going to happen next when J.D. drew the walk. The Blue Jays prepared for me by going to the 'pen and bringing in a right-hander named Kevin Gregg.

The problem for me was that their manager, Cito Gaston, might have thought that Gregg was coming in to face me, but my manager didn't agree.

"David! David! David!"

I could hear a commotion behind me, a bunch of screaming voices. I was at home plate, digging in already. My first thought was, *Oh shit, what happened?* Nothing *had* happened. Something *was* happening. Tito was pinch-hitting for me. In April. With the bases loaded. That was bad enough, and I didn't agree with it. What made it worse was the way he did it. I'm standing up there getting ready to hit, and he makes the last-second decision to bring in Mikey to replace me. It was embarrassing. Man, was it ever embarrassing.

There weren't many fans in the park that night, somewhere around 15,000. I wouldn't think that they were all watching me, but it felt that way. The NESN cameras were there, seemingly zooming in from every possible angle. I felt like I had a camera guy in my pocket. You know how that angle is from ESPN when you hit a home run? When the camera is in your face? That's exactly how I felt.

I knew what they wanted, and I wasn't going to give it to them. Everybody watching in Toronto and at home in New England was expecting me to go fucking crazy, and I did. But I did it behind the scenes. I was angry. I was also trying to be smart. If I went off on TV, I knew how that would play with the public. The clip would be shown 50 times by midnight, and it would be an invitation for even more people to talk shit about me. No thanks.

As I walked through the dugout and to the tunnel, it started to sink in what Tito had just done. It was disrespectful. I always thought he understood who I was as a player and as a man, but it was clear to me that he didn't understand as much as I thought he did.

Our relationship, which had been really good for five years, lost its core of trust that night. I knew we'd never be the same going forward. His move was an announcement to the baseball world. He didn't think I was the same player anymore. If he'd thought my April struggles were due to a slow start, he would have left me in there. He took me out because he didn't think I could do the job.

Once in that tunnel, with no cameras in sight, I went off. I threw my bat, my helmet, my gloves, my elbow pad. Anything that could be thrown, I threw it. No one came near me, and no one wanted to talk. Especially not Tito. And I didn't want to talk to him in that moment either. He could have said something before it all happened, but he chose not to.

I finally made it to the clubhouse and took a shower. I dressed quickly and waited for the very last out of the game, which we won. As soon as it was over, I hustled out of there without talking to the media. It was another smart decision. If I had said even half of what I was thinking and feeling that night, I would have given the critics their stories for the rest of the year, if not the rest of my career. I'm not joking. There are some long memories among fans and media. If I had said something crazy after the game, the comment would have been replayed continuously, living on forever.

Still, I wasn't all that sweet the next day. One of the radio reporters, Jonny Miller, came up to me and said, "Why did you leave before the end of the game?" He was throwing out a false story to me, and I was already pissed about the night before. Bad timing on his part. I told Jonny to fuck off. I told him that he should have known that I'm not stupid, I wouldn't leave a game before it ended, and maybe he should have checked with his sources before peddling that garbage. If I had left before the game, a bad situation would have gotten worse.

And yes, as far as I was concerned, this was bad. There had been no warning, no heads-up, nothing. The minute I struggle, you're going to turn your back on me? Where's the loyalty? Where's the fairness?

Tito did what he did and felt what he felt, but there was another factor in his decision in Toronto. You've got everyone, from the media to the front office, in your ear saying, "He's done, he's done." Hearing that every day, probably 90 percent of managers would have done the same thing that Tito did. The other 10 percent of managers who will take it in the ass for you, they're rare. And many of them are making decisions in small markets where there's no daily media agenda to contend with.

In a lot of ways, it's the media in New England who run the ball club. Once they start hounding you, in print, on the radio, on TV, it's constant. You can't be on the fence. Either you're against the media or you give in to what they want. Looking at it that way, as the season progressed, I stopped blaming Tito alone for that night in Toronto. He'd felt that pressure to do what he was always being asked about.

A few weeks after Toronto, the commentary began to change about me and our team. Earlier in the year, people were saying I couldn't catch up to a fastball, which I found funny. I wish pitchers had felt the same way and challenged me with them inside. They didn't because they understood how much I loved that pitch. My wife used to watch me study video in the off-season, studying at times when she thought we should have been shopping or something. She would ask why I was looking so carefully at the video and I'd give her a simple answer: I'm hunting for mistakes — anytime they throw 'em, I hit 'em.

By early July, I had hit my share of mistakes. I was a regular in the lineup again. At that point, I had hit 17 home runs and driven in 54, and had a slugging percentage of .566. I was selected to my sixth All-Star team and asked to compete in my fourth Home Run Derby. I didn't hear anyone calling sports talk radio anymore, saying that I should be released. Our team was 49-32 on July 3, after a win over Baltimore. It was the halfway point of our season, and we were just a half-game out of first place in the division.

Those were all good things. The issues were with our injuries.

Dustin Pedroia had been having a great season, but he broke a bone in his left foot and had to go on the disabled list. Jacoby Ellsbury was already on the DL with broken ribs. Víctor Martínez had a fractured thumb. Clay Buchholz had a hyperextended knee. We were a high-payroll team with a lot of depth, but that was too much missing talent to ignore.

Our slide actually began after that Baltimore win, the week before the All-Star Game in Anaheim. It was a bad week. We lost five out of seven, all to divisional opponents, and went from a half-game behind to five out at the break. We got swept by first-place Tampa, with their win in the final game coming from 24-year-old David Price. As I'd expected, he had become an All-Star and Cy Young Award candidate. With Price leading a rotation stocked with pitchers under 30, and with all our injuries, it was going to be challenging for us to catch the Rays.

I knew I'd have a lot of time to think about the near and distant future during the second half of the season. But at the All-Star break, all I could do was smile and think of the people who'd had to eat their words. And my manager, who had to change his lineup to include me every day. Three months earlier, fans and media in Boston had wanted my ass to be released. Now here I was in California on an All-Star team. Not only that, I'd advanced to the final round of the Home Run Derby, where I was facing off against Hanley Ramírez, the former Red Sox minor leaguer. I beat Hanley head to head. He was a good kid. He told me that I was like a father to him in baseball, and that he was happy that I'd won a contest that, although symbolic, said what I still was. A hitter. A home run hitter. After all the doubts.

It's too bad our team didn't have a similar turnaround story. We were good, but with Tampa and the Yankees in our division, it took more than that. We won 89 games. The Rays and Yankees made the playoffs, though, with 96 and 95 wins.

• • •

It had been an educational year for me, in every way. Instead of business running away from me, I continued to get more opportunities. I'd opened a suburban restaurant, Big Papi's Grille, and now I was in talks for another restaurant partnership downtown.

My view of baseball politics had sharpened in 2009 and 2010 as well. I had gone through hell the previous July and August, but the positive in that experience was that it woke me up to the flaws in the system. The *New York Times* report was an example of how twisted things could be behind the scenes. There was nothing fair about my name being on that list. Every other player whose name had been up in a PED allegation before knew what they tested positive for. Every single player but me. What did that tell me? That someone felt there had been too much focus on PEDs and the Yankees and it was time for the Red Sox to be mentioned too. Or that someone was just aiming to hurt my image.

I was confident then and I'm confident now: no one can prove that I tested positive for something, because it didn't happen.

As for the business of playing baseball, the year reinforced a few lessons for me, ones I've not only learned myself but that I tell young players who ask for advice. I tell them, and remind myself, that you have to be confident and savvy when playing this game. Don't let anyone define who you are and what you're capable of. If I'd listened to everyone in the spring of 2010, I would have just put my head down and gone home. Instead, I finished with 32 home runs, 36 doubles, and 102 runs batted in. Back to bangin'.

Look, the reason we play this game is not just because we love it. It's also an opportunity to give ourselves and our families a better situation. We're looking to the future, so we have to be smart. We have to make good decisions, and sometimes we have to swallow our pride and play along with what the organization wants.

Sometimes.

My contract was up at the end of the 2010 season, and I didn't see myself the way the Red Sox did. I thought my value was higher than they did. So while sometimes you have to play along, at other times you just have to stand up and fight on principle. Theo Epstein showed me that when he left the Red Sox in 2005. Five years later, I was ready to fight him on what I believed was rightfully mine.

15

Paper Tigers

My agent had some calls to make on my behalf, during and after the 2010 Red Sox season. He was supposed to be exploring specifics: what would the Red Sox be willing to pay to keep me in Boston beyond 2011? Once he'd completed his homework, he hesitated to share what he had learned.

"I almost don't want to tell you what their offer was," he said.

The "they" he was talking about included general manager Theo Epstein and his staff. They had the choice of picking up a 2011 team option, worth $12.5 million, or signing me to a multiyear deal. I was a few weeks away from turning 35, and they wanted me to be with the team into my late thirties. So did I. It seemed that we were going in the same direction until I pressed my agent for details of the Red Sox proposal.

Instead of the option, he told me, their on-the-table suggestion was worth two years and $16 million. I asked him to repeat what he'd said, because it couldn't have been what I had heard. That could not possibly be right. They basically wanted to buy an extra year for $3.5 million. It occurred to me that these were the types of behind-the-scenes things that fans would never know. In negotiating with an athlete, the team had all the power, at least when it came to perception. If the player didn't accept the offer, no matter how imbalanced the terms, then he was greedy. Ungrateful. Selfish.

I was already sick of this routine. I knew it was going to be a big trading and free agency season for the Red Sox. They were going to be aggressive, for many reasons: we'd been swept from the play-offs in 2009 and missed them altogether in 2010; NESN's ratings had dropped; there had been a sellout streak since 2003, but anyone could see there were more and more empty seats popping up at Fenway; and as a big-market team, the Red Sox had cash to spend.

I had heard rumors about who they wanted. Carl Crawford, a left fielder for Tampa, was a free agent. He was fast against other teams and the fastest man in the world against us. He'd always given us hell as a base stealer, so I was sure the Red Sox would call him. They also liked Adrián González. He was a high-average, power-hitting first baseman in San Diego, and Theo had been trying to pry him loose from the Padres for years. If either one of them was going to come to Boston, the team would have to spend a ton. And honestly, this was where I always ran into an issue with the financial thinking of the Red Sox.

Would I have liked to have Crawford and González on my side? Of course. I'm a winner. I liked to play with winners. There's no way a team can be in position for a World Series title without a bunch of good, winning players around. My problem was that every time it was my turn to talk about contracts, I damn near had to wrestle every dollar and cent away from the team. And whenever a story would get out that I was looking to get paid, people were looking at me like, "Oh, here comes David Ortiz again . . ." It really pissed me off. Sometimes I just wanted to shout, "Yo! Wake the fuck up. I'm the best weapon you have, but I'm not the best-paid weapon you have. And I should be."

It was an aspect of playing in Boston that I didn't understand.

Maybe the disconnect was in the way the Red Sox, and some of the public, viewed me as a player compared to the way I viewed myself. Their words and their actions told me that they thought I couldn't carry a team anymore. The talk show hosts and callers thought it and said it; I heard them for the first two months of 2010. The columnists thought it. I read their articles about how I should accept being a part-time player, at best, or maybe think about walking away from the game. My manager, Tito Francona, thought it. He turned his back on me in April, before we knew anything about the season. Although we eventually talked and had a working relationship again, I never forgot that when Tito really felt he needed to win that game, he didn't think I could do it for him. And with the sorry contract offer, Theo Epstein told me that he thought it as well. He was treating me like shit with that proposal.

I knew that I was still an elite hitter, even if they didn't. My work habits never changed, and neither did my self-awareness. If I couldn't get it done anymore, if I couldn't catch up to a fastball, I would know that before anyone else. And I would admit it. I sure would know it before some sports columnist, who had no idea what it was like to dig in against the best pitchers in the world and try to hit a baseball traveling 98 miles per hour. With all respect, I'd know it before Tito and Theo too.

It didn't take me long to reject the offer, if you want to call it that, from the Red Sox. They picked up the option, so I was under contract for the 2011 season and then I'd be a free agent. It crossed my mind that the Red Sox were just trying to be good businessmen and not be on the hook for a long contract with me at my age. Fine. But if that was the way they were going, their negotiating style didn't make sense.

When you consider everything, I was the most underpaid player the organization ever had. Why do I say that? Because of what I provided, happily, besides baseball. At this point, I was the face of the team, and everyone in every department knew it. They would ask me for something and the answer was usually yes. It wasn't just about getting hits and winning championships. That whole organization was my second family, so I would wind up doing something for the guys in the parking lot, for the clubhouse crew, for marketing and promotions, I'd respond to TV requests, I'd talk to kids. Ask anyone there. They wouldn't let me breathe. I did it all, and I was happy to do it. It's just who I am. Some players have the mind-set that, hey, I'm just a baseball player and fuck off about everything else. Not me. I was involved in every aspect of the organization.

Then the contract situation would come up. They'd talk about me as a DH, when they and I both knew I was much more than that to them. It was predictable. I'd say publicly and privately, "If there's one player in this organization who has earned every single dollar, I'm sorry, but it's me."

It was funny that my speaking up seemed to hurt some people's feelings, after all I'd given to the Red Sox. Was I so insignificant that I couldn't talk and think about myself for a minute?

I wasn't surprised when the conversation about my contract didn't last long. They picked up my option in November. By December, they were back to their free-spending selves. I'd seen it play out, time and again, without anyone seeming to keep track of what they'd done. They'd overpay players and then *hope* they could adjust to Boston. They'd underpay me, *knowing* that there was nothing about playing in Boston that I couldn't handle.

As expected, they signed Crawford. What no one, including Crawford, expected was the size of the contract. They gave him $142 million guaranteed, or $20 million per year over seven years. Crawford told me straight up that all that money came out of nowhere. One day he said to me, "Damn, Papi. I was expecting $80 to $90 million, and they came to me with $142 million right out of the gate. I was driving and almost crashed when my agent told me. My agent was like, 'The Red Sox have $142 million for yo' ass.' And I was like, 'Who do I have to kill?'"

Once the Yankees had dinner with Crawford, the Red Sox panicked and overpaid him. That's what I believed. They were desperate to get him. I was happy to have Crawford, but frustrated with Theo. Theo wasn't done. He also traded four prospects, Anthony Rizzo and Casey Kelly the most highly regarded among them, to the Padres for González. I loved watching González hit. We had completely different styles, but I knew that he was the kind of person who would want to sit and exchange ideas about the game. He had hit 40 home runs two years earlier, and with a chance to play nearly 100 games between Fenway, Yankee Stadium, and Camden Yards, some people thought he'd match that with the Red Sox. Maybe he'd even pass it and top 50.

Like Crawford, one thing he wouldn't have to worry about was his next contract. He was also given a long-term deal — seven years for $154 million. That came out to an average of $22 million per season. I wasn't stupid. Even though these players were just being given the money that I had been fighting for, I knew what their presence meant. Our lineup was going to be loaded. There wasn't one area where we were lacking. We had two speedy outfielders in Crawford and Jacoby Ellsbury. González and I had the power covered. Dustin Pedroia was back from his foot injury, and he could do everything. One through nine, we had hitters who could wear out a staff.

As for our pitching, I felt it was the best top-to-bottom staff we'd had since I arrived in Boston. Our top starters were Josh Beckett, Jon Lester, John Lackey, and Clay Buchholz. Three of those four had started and won the deciding game of a World Series. Our bullpen was stacked. We had Jonathan Papelbon as our closer, and a kid with an incredible mix of pitches, Daniel Bard, setting him up. The only thing that was missing from our staff was the pitching coach from the previous four seasons. John Farrell, who commanded a lot of respect among the pitchers, had left for Toronto to manage the Blue Jays.

I was excited about our team, and so were fans and reporters. At the end of March, just before our first road trip of the season, the *Boston Herald* had a headline that summed up what a lot of people were thinking: "Best Team Ever." I didn't know about that, but I thought we'd blow the division away. Physically, I felt great. And from what I could see, so did a lot of my teammates.

I'd hit just .222 against left-handed pitching in 2010. I'd hit 32 home runs, but just two came off lefties. I needed help going into the season, so one day at the batting cage I approached my new teammate, González. I'm more of a pull hitter than González, and I thought I was trying to pull the ball too much against lefties. Watching González gave me some ideas. I asked him what his plan was when a lefty was bearing down on him.

"I give them the inside of the plate," he explained. "And I focus on all pitches on the outer third."

I smiled and shook my head.

"That makes a lot of sense," I replied. "They don't pitch me inside, and I'm pulling everything. But everything I'm pulling is outside. What I need to do is just stay on the pitch and go with it."

It was simple, yet it sparked something in me. I knew then that I'd be better against lefties than I'd been in a while.

When the 2011 season started, we weren't prepared for it. I'm not sure why. Maybe it was because a lot of players were trying to do too much. Maybe it was the pressure of being named one of the best teams of all time before we'd even played a game. I don't know. We just weren't ready.

We went to Texas and got swept, and followed that by getting swept in Cleveland. We came home for our opener against the Yankees and won two out of three, but then we faced the Rays at home and we got swept again. Four series played, three sweeps. We were a lot of things, but we were not the Best Team Ever. Far from it.

At 2-10, it was hard to say that any one big thing was the reason for the terrible start. We didn't know it at the time, but our clubhouse reflected the entire organization: many agendas, many directions. The level of dysfunction would be apparent much later in the season, and I wasn't above contributing to some of it myself. But that was for the summer. In the spring, the issues were the definition of roles and the comfort level in Boston. Theo had grown up about a mile from Fenway and understood the psyche of Red Sox fans. He was one of them, and so he knew how the demanding baseball culture could eat up and spit out certain personality types. That's why I was surprised over the years by his interest in some players who clearly had a problem with Boston's intensity.

Crawford, for example, was not comfortable. The pressure he put on himself to perform to the enormous contract was part of it, and for a while he didn't know where he should fit in the lineup. Leadoff? Number two? Number six? Put the ball on the ground and use your legs? Or use the relative power that resulted in a career-high 19 home runs in 2010? He never settled in, and he didn't look like the same player he had been in Tampa.

González, meanwhile, was a great hitter. He always had a plan at the plate, and he made hitting to all fields look effortless. He was a West Coast guy, though, and getting used to the urgency and brashness of the East Coast — whether it was driving, talking, or reporting — was an adjustment for him. Both he and Crawford were All-Star players, so the hope was that talent would overshadow everything else.

That's what started to happen in June and July, when we put together a couple of impressive runs. We had a 14-2 stretch in June. Just before the All-Star break, we went 10-1. We still had some fight in us. I mean that literally.

On a Friday night in Baltimore, we got off to a dream start against the Orioles. It was an eight-run first inning, so their manager, Buck Showalter, went to his bullpen early. I'd personally never had a problem with Showalter, although earlier in the year he'd been critical of the Red Sox and our high payroll. At one point, he called for reliever Kevin Gregg, a pitcher who had never pitched me inside before. My only significant history with Gregg had come the year before, in Toronto. He was the pitcher I didn't have the opportunity to face because Tito pinch-hit for me. In Baltimore in 2011, I knew something was up when Gregg kept trying to throw in to me, including one pitch that came close to my face. That's when he pissed me off. Any baseball player will tell you not to mess around with pitches around his head. I dug in and thought, *It's on, baby. If you hit me, I know it's on purpose. And I'm coming for that ass.* He was trying to hit me and didn't succeed. He threw a pitch that I popped up for an easy out, and as I was running down the line I heard him say, "Run, motherfucker, run!"

That was it. I wasn't going to be talked to like that by anybody. I charged the mound and threw a huge left at Gregg, and he threw a wild right at me. We both missed, fortunately. We're both big men — he's six-six and about 250 pounds — and we could have caused some damage.

The benches cleared, and things calmed down quickly. I knew it was Gregg who threw the pitches, but I was certain that the directions came from Showalter. I never said anything to him afterward, and he didn't say anything to me. Most players on both teams moved on from the incident. But every time we played Baltimore, there was something about Showalter that made me feel that he never did. That wouldn't be confirmed until several years later, when his true character would be revealed in an embarrassing way.

We were red-hot in July, so no one talked about our early season slump anymore. Some of the core issues that we had as an organization still lingered, though. They were just concealed by all the wins.

I was grateful for many things. We were in first place, I was selected to my seventh All-Star Game, and I was back to crushing left-handed pitching. I had 19 home runs at the break, along with 55 runs batted in, and an overall .304 batting average. González's tip had really paid off for me. I was hitting for a higher average and slugging percentage against lefties than righties. I was one of six Red Sox All-Stars, along with González, Beckett, Lester, Ellsbury, and Youkilis.

We continued to play well after the break, well into early August, although there were some minor eruptions. One of them was mine.

We played the Indians at Fenway and won 4–3 on an Ellsbury walk-off home run. In the first inning of the game, I thought I drove in two runs with a line drive to left field. I hit that ball so hard that the left fielder couldn't field it but could only block it. González was on third and scored easily. Youkilis was running on contact and would have scored no matter what happened. The official scorer that night disagreed. He said the second run scored due to an error. The next day one of my teammates said to me, "Can you believe they scored that an error last night?" I was hot then, and started asking people where Tito was. I was told that he was in a room on the mezzanine level of Fenway, next to our weight room. I walked in hot, pointing and cussing. There was a problem, though: he was in the middle of a press conference.

The entire Red Sox media corps, representing all of New England, saw my anger and heard my complaint. Tito said he would talk with me later, and I walked away. Now, you might be wondering, why get that upset over one silly RBI? I'll explain it this way: I come from nothing. And fucking with somebody's job is not my thing. I respect everyone that respects me. If you don't respect me, I'm not going to respect you. That's the way I am. But if you respect me, I will always respect you. Simple.

But I truly believed that the scorekeepers at Fenway made a lot of mistakes. I didn't know if the scorekeepers were always the same people, but what I did know was that we were screwed by them dozens of times. I was just fed up with it that day. It was as if I remembered all the slights at the same time and it pushed me over the edge. I remembered a game against the Orioles when I hit a ball in the hole. Rafael Palmeiro was playing first base at the time. He dove for the ball and grabbed it, but couldn't throw me out because the pitcher didn't cover the base. I was safe at first. The scorekeeper called that an error. What, you score a mental mistake as an error? Everything was always against the hitter, and that was my livelihood. That was my pride.

In retrospect, there were a lot of things on my mind besides the loss of the RBI. But that was the one incident too many, the one that had me saying to myself, *I can't do this shit no more.* Eventually, I'd be able to step back and assess all the things, some life-changing and some career-altering, that were on my heart and mind then. I wasn't thinking in a big-picture way that day.

They eventually changed the error and gave me that RBI. If I hadn't gotten mad . . . if I hadn't expressed my anger . . . if I hadn't fought, what would have happened? I was in my contract year, and I knew how the Red Sox viewed things. I knew my numbers could be thrown at me come negotiation time. All I did was hit, man. If I didn't hit, well, in their eyes I hadn't done shit. Listen, when I was hitting .230, everybody was talking trash about me. When I wasn't hitting well, it was, "Oh, Big Papi is done. Big Papi is this, Big Papi is that." So when I worked hard to get a hit and they gave it an error, in my book, that was a minus.

Tito understood that part of it. He was a baseball player too. He understood how hard it is to get an RBI. One year I got 99 RBIs. It's not 100. When you hit .299, it's not .300. You've got to think the way management does. Ninety-nine doesn't sound as lovely as 102 or 103.

I'll admit that I was thinking about my future during the 2011 season. And I was not alone. One day in August, out of nowhere, there was an ESPN report that Theo Epstein was interested in leaving the Red Sox to become president of the Chicago Cubs. I hadn't thought about Theo leaving since he had done it six years earlier. One of the Red Sox owners, Tom Werner, denied the report. I wasn't so sure. There was a lot of uncertainty in the franchise, top to bottom. Theo was looking to leave. Tito was in the final year of his contract, waiting to see if the team would pick up his option. I was going to be a free agent, and so was Papelbon.

Some major decisions had to be made before the end of the year, and no one was paying attention to them until some minimal slides turned into an avalanche. One of the things that became symbolic of our collapsing season was, of all things, chicken and beer.

That was not a controversial phrase on the last day of August. That night, in a game started by Beckett, we beat the Yankees at Fenway. Our record was 83-52, and we led our division by a game and a half. There wasn't even a discussion of whether we'd make the playoffs with a month left in the season. We just knew we were going to make it. Our lead was too comfortable. We were too good.

The next 24 hours seemed to change all of that, though.

We began September with a loss, and then every day it seemed like another flaw was exposed. As a staff, we had pitched well all year. But one of our starters, John Lackey, had pitched most of the season with a torn rotator cuff. No one in the media knew it. His earned run average was well over six. When we were winning, the fans didn't like his performance, but there were other good things about the team to think about. But when our disastrous first week of September included a Lackey start where he gave up six runs in five innings, he became a bigger target.

Even after that bad week, with our record at 85-58, we were still seven games ahead of Tampa for the wild card with just 19 games left in the season. On September 9, we took our 85 wins to Tampa for a three-game series. When the series was over, we left Tampa with . . . 85 wins. Now we were just four games ahead of them with 16 to play, and we were a mess. Our starting pitching had caved. That dominant setup man from earlier in the season, Daniel Bard, suddenly lost it. He'd allowed four total runs in July and August. He gave up six runs in the first three innings he pitched in September.

It was falling apart, from all directions. Even normal things that weren't a big deal eventually were viewed as a big deal. Like chicken and beer.

We'd always had chicken and beer in the clubhouse. Having chicken and beer in the clubhouse was like playing the National Anthem before games. It was there. It was always going to be there. Some of our starting pitchers were eating it in the clubhouse during the game. It wasn't a big deal for the starters because they weren't playing. If I ever got hungry during the game and I wasn't playing, do you think I'd wait for the game to be over? No. I'd eat.

But we were getting our asses beat at the end of the season, and it was going to have to be blamed on something. What was once a comfortable lead had shrunk all the way to a tie at the end of the year. All we had to do was beat the last-place team in our division, the Orioles, to have some type of postseason. Either we'd get in outright as the wild card or we'd have to play a one-game playoff with Tampa.

But in one of the strangest seasons of my life, at any level, the collapse was complete. We went 7-20 in September, one of the worst meltdowns by a contender in baseball history. It was like we got smacked by the baseball gods. *You think you have it figured out? Watch what we're going to do to you.* I'd been around for a while, and I'd never experienced anything like it.

I've heard a lot of people give reasons for why it happened, from a lack of pitching, to my interruption of Tito's press conference, to chicken and beer. I don't think any of those things were the reason.

I honestly don't know why so many great players couldn't come together and figure out how to get into the playoffs that year.

I did know this, though: someone always pays for a year like that. Sometimes the scapegoat is a player, and sometimes it's the manager. This time it was the manager. With a twist. The Red Sox decided not to pick up Tito's option, which basically meant they fired him. I wasn't surprised at all. I don't root for anyone to lose their job, but I'm also realistic. With our team playing like that and Tito's contract being up, it was easy to see what would happen. I thought Tito did a great job in his time with the Red Sox, and he was good to me, for the most part. We developed more of a business relationship after that night in Toronto, and so that's how I looked at his firing. It was an inevitable business move. Soon after he left, Theo Epstein resigned and headed to Chicago for more money and a promotion.

It felt like the entire organization was vulnerable. Four years earlier, in Denver, I had seen the Red Sox at our best. We won the Series that night, and I couldn't have been happier professionally. Now, after the 2011 season, we couldn't have been lower. After an accusatory *Boston Globe* article, I wasn't even sure there was a "we" anymore. The article was full of rumors, finger-pointing, and backstabbing from anonymous sources. One of these sources talked about the chicken and beer in the clubhouse and suggested that our pitching staff didn't work hard enough. Another source took some personal swipes at Tito and claimed, among other things, that he was too distracted by his personal life to be a good manager. Yet another claim was that our team was fractured and unwilling to put the work in to be great. It was a mess. Those types of stories never represent the entire accurate picture of a season. But with that said, somebody was talking to the media. Who was doing that? Whoever it was — or whoever they were — had no concept of teamwork. No matter how bad things are, you don't sell out your family.

As bad as that article was, it was a preview of things to come in our organization. We were going to go from bad to worse.

It was a chaotic time for me, in both my personal life and my baseball life. One of my best friends was to be married in January 2012, and he asked me to be a groomsman in his wedding. It was ironic because he was going to be at the beginning of his marriage as I appeared to be at the end of mine. And when I tried to escape that thought and just think about baseball, there was no peace there either. When the Red Sox hired Bobby Valentine as the new manager, I got phone call after phone call from players who had been around him. They all said the same thing:

Good luck.

16

Breaks and Rebellions

I had never met Bobby Valentine before 2011. I'd heard of him, seen him on TV, and remembered that he was the guy who'd put on a fake mustache to avoid being recognized and thrown out of a game. But I didn't know the man, so that left me with an interesting decision at the end of the year: Should I listen to my friends, or pretend that I'd never heard a word they said?

Everyone I knew was unimpressed with Valentine, the new manager of the Red Sox. He was hired in late November 2011, and the negative reaction from my baseball friends was instant. There were the sarcastic "good luck" messages. There were ominous warnings to get ready. Some even suggested that, at 36 years old, I probably wanted to retire rather than play for someone like him.

Valentine hadn't managed in the United States in a decade, although he had been a managerial star in Japan. He had spent a lot of time around the game as an ESPN analyst, and he was full of opinions on how the game should be played.

I'm a person who has been able to get along with a range of personalities, pretty much everybody, so I tried to block out all the information I had. I tried not to think about the fact that the Red Sox never asked my opinion on players they were thinking about signing or managers they wanted to hire. They weren't interested in sharing, even though I felt I could have helped many times with things I knew as a veteran player on the team, things they seemed not to know. I found out on the news, just like everyone else, that Valentine was our new manager. I did some research and learned that there was basically one person in the organization, team president Larry Lucchino, who really wanted to hire Valentine. That was it. One person. Still, I'd been a peacemaker in many situations. And I had to perform regardless of who was managing. How bad could Bobby V really be?

In early December, he decided to come to my golf tournament in the Dominican. I thought it was a nice gesture, and I spoke with him briefly. He was cool. I was a free agent, and Bobby told me that he was hopeful that I'd return to the Red Sox. Theo Epstein wasn't negotiating the deals anymore, as he had moved on to Chicago, but the tone of the talks was the same. Ben Cherington was the new general manager, and it was frustrating to deal with someone else who acted like he didn't know what I could do. How many times do you need me to give you 30 home runs and 100 runs batted in before you understand that's who I am? I wanted to be paid what I was worth, on a long-term deal. The numbers the Red Sox were using weren't even close to mine. We agreed to go to arbitration, and just before we got there we settled on a one-year contract for $14.5 million.

At least Cherington was consistent with Epstein. Neither one of them made getting a deal done easy. But no matter how tough it was to talk money, it didn't come close to what was in front of me, coming from all directions, in 2012.

The drama began almost immediately in spring training. I couldn't find the calm Bobby I'd seen in the Dominican. I remember fighting the thought, very early, *We're going to have an absolutely terrible year.*

It was all about him in the spring. It was as if he wanted to prove how smart he was by running us through all these drills he'd used while managing in Japan, drills we had never done before. Come on. This was major league baseball. In the United States of America. Everybody else playing baseball around the world wanted to be like us. Bobby was in his own bubble, and I just wanted to get him out of it and tell him, "Fuck you and the way you want to train and teach people how to play the game that you learned in Japan."

He asked for a lot of changes, including some that were completely unnecessary. One of the more ridiculous ones was having players hit grounders to each other. I thought that was funny, especially for me. The Red Sox weren't paying me to hit grounders; I was there to hit balls to the moon. But that drill wasn't the deal-breaker for me or the team. There was another drill that essentially caused him to lose his new team before we even left Florida. That's not an exaggeration. He made it difficult for players to have his back, although I tried my hardest privately and every time I was asked about him publicly.

The problem was not that his drills were new. The bigger issue was how he expected players who had been in the big leagues a long time to immediately do things his way without any missteps. I wasn't sure, at that time, if that was truly his personality or if someone was telling him to act that way. There had been a lot of conversations about our team the year before, and how our lack of accountability led to our September collapse. Maybe Bobby was told to come in and boss around full-grown men. Maybe the Red Sox wanted to hire a daddy, not a manager.

One day we were doing his drills and the shit hit the fan. We were hitting pop-ups, and Bobby had said that he didn't want infielders to say, "I've got it, I've got it . . ." He thought that was an unreliable way of calling off a teammate because, in a noisy stadium, the player who's being called off might not hear his teammate taking control. Well, all players have habits. Many of those habits lead big league players to the majors and keep them there. And in American baseball, most infielders taking the play say, "I got it."

So when our shortstop, Mike Aviles, got under a ball, he instinctively said, "I got it." Bobby snapped. It was unlike anything I had ever seen in the majors. He went off on Aviles, cussing and verbally tearing him down in front of everyone. Listen, if it had been me, I would have gone up to him, right in front of the fans, and dropped a punch. Aviles was not his son or his grandson. He was a grown man, a major league baseball player who had worked hard to get there and who had fielding habits that had helped him do that. For him to all of a sudden have to change that, well, there should have been some patience.

After that workout, I talked with Dustin Pedroia and Adrián González. We decided to meet with Bobby in his office and attempt to tell him how he was being perceived. It was a waste of time. We tried reasoning with him, and it was like communicating with a wall. All he did was roll his eyes and look everywhere but at us. It could not have been more obvious that he didn't care what we had to say. We left his office shaking our heads.

I was competitive enough to think that we could win a bunch of games despite Bobby's ego. We still had Josh Beckett and Jon Lester at the top of our rotation. Even though Jonathan Papelbon had left for Philadelphia in free agency, I felt that we had an extremely talented closer to replace him, Mark Melancon, who was just 27 years old. If we used him properly, we'd be all right in the back of the bullpen. Our lineup had many of the same players from the year before, when we topped the majors in runs, on-base percentage, and slugging percentage. One guy who was with us but wouldn't be in the lineup was Carl Crawford. He had had wrist surgery, and he was going to miss at least half of the season.

It didn't take long for me to realize I'd been too optimistic. And when I say not long, I mean the first series of the season. We opened in Detroit and were swept by the Tigers. It was impossible to ignore the comments from my teammates about Bobby's managing, how he made decisions that didn't make sense, and how generally clueless and distant he was. The next stop on our trip was Toronto. On the flight there, I experienced a first in my career.

Bobby's seat was in the middle of the plane, and the players were in the back. That day I was near the front of our section. I remember looking up and seeing a line of my teammates walking toward me. They were pissed. I was like, "Whoa, whoa. What's going on?" They said, "We want that motherfucker fired before the airplane lands."

I had never seen anything like that. I didn't know what they might have done if they had gotten to him, but I felt it was way too early in the season for that kind of takeover. He was aggravating as hell, arrogant, and disrespectful, but I felt that we needed to try our best to support him.

I knew all the big payroll guys — Lester, González, Beckett, Crawford — wanted him fired. That feeling hadn't changed two weeks later when we were just 4-8. After batting practice, before a game at Fenway against the Yankees, I called a players-only meeting. I remember things got heated, and I almost got into a fistfight with my boy Beckett, who I love. My point during the meeting was that, yes, the manager was terrible, but we weren't hitting or pitching very well either. It was hard to make a case against Bobby when we sucked ourselves. It got uncomfortable with Beckett because I called him out. He knew how much I respected him and believed in his talent. I told him I didn't think he was as focused as he should have been, and not only was it affecting his own pitching, it was trickling down to Lester and Buchholz, who both looked up to him.

I pushed his buttons on purpose. I wanted to light a fire under him and everyone he came across. I wanted to get everyone going, myself included. I admit that I was afraid of having a miserable season, and not just because I wanted to win so badly. If life with my second family, my baseball family, was out of order, then that meant there was no peace anywhere.

My own family life was going through changes. Tiffany and I had been together for 16 years, but we had agreed that we couldn't keep living the way we were. Things were falling apart for many reasons. It was hard to pinpoint exactly what it was, but we weren't the same. Somewhere along the way, our normal lives had gotten lost in the celebrity life. That wasn't us, although we didn't have the perspective at the time to correct the problems. We decided to separate and start the divorce process.

Tiffany is one of the best people I have ever met, an incredible wife, mother, and friend. The decision was painful but, we thought, for the best. We talked about living our lives together, for the kids, but we would physically live in different places. We'd bought a home in Weston and were part of a special neighborhood. The neighbors didn't just wave and disappear into their houses. People cared and looked out for one another. Sometimes I'd look around and be amazed by the contrast between the life I'd had growing up and the comfortable life we'd been able to provide for our kids. I still loved Tiffany deeply. But we weren't getting along well at all, and I moved out. I got a place in Chestnut Hill, on Boylston Street, and either the kids would come there or I'd go to the house in Weston to see them. They'd still come to games, and I made sure I was still a strong presence in their lives.

Tiffany's character shone through when the lawyers got involved. She was loving, even as we were separating. She had a lawyer who wanted to emphasize my celebrity status, so he went in hard, asking for everything he could. But Tiffany was composed, and she made it clear that she didn't want anything extra. She wanted a peaceful transition and requested a straightforward split of assets. One of the brighter moments during this dark time was when she commented that she knew I'd continue to be a good father and provider.

Without a doubt, it was the worst season of my career. Each day, nothing got better. Not my separation from Tiffany, and not the tense and irrational atmosphere that Bobby created in the clubhouse. As a team, we had some weeks when it would look like we were turning a corner. We won six games in a row shortly after our players-only meeting in April. In May we had another small streak, five in a row. I remember the final game in that streak was won by Beckett. He was great that night, shutting out Seattle on just a few hits and nine strikeouts. When he came out of the game, I was one of the first people congratulating him in the dugout. I knew we'd be all right, whether it was Josh and me or any of the players on our team.

Our manager, though, couldn't help himself. He kept getting in the way.

The simplest way I can put it is that he didn't treat people well. That's what it came down to. He dismissed anyone who he thought was beneath him. He didn't get a chance to hire all his own coaches, and I think he held it against the coaches themselves. We had a bench coach named Tim Bogar. He was an intelligent guy, and I really liked him. He tried to give Bobby a scouting report on a player, and Bobby just tore into him for no reason. The point was to work as a team and help each other get better, but that was missing from him. He even called a meeting, with the entire team, and accused his coaches of backstabbing him.

Another time, when we were playing the Cubs in Chicago, his target was Melancon. It wasn't as bad as the way he attacked Aviles, but it was close. Melancon hadn't pitched well, and as usual, Bobby overreacted to something that a player hadn't done on purpose. Bobby played in the majors. He should have known. Did he really think a guy wanted to perform poorly? Did he believe his screaming and sarcasm would make things better? I remember seeing Melancon's face afterward, and it was tomato red. I felt so bad for the kid. I pulled him aside and told him that he was a great pitcher and not to be discouraged by Bobby. I needed him to know that this experience was the exception and that the best baseball teams didn't operate this way. I could see what was happening. Melancon would be a good closer for someone, but never for Bobby Valentine.

Eventually, in July, we all collapsed.

For me, it started with an injury. Despite the instability in my life and in the clubhouse, I was having a great season at the plate. I had made my third straight All-Star Game after being called washed up in 2009 and 2010. The advice from González on how to approach lefties was continuing to pay off, and for the second year in a row my average was higher against them than against righties. It was a good time to be in a contract year. About a week after the All-Star Game, at home against the White Sox, González hit a home run and I was on base. As I made the turn at second, I felt a shot in my right foot. It was a pain so sharp that as I got to third I was convinced that I'd torn something. Later I was told that I'd been fortunate. I had almost torn my Achilles tendon. The doctors said it would be wise to sit out for a while.

In the meantime, my teammates fought on without me on the field and fought against Bobby off of it. There was a meeting with ownership in New York to get him fired. He was terrible, and everyone knew it. Even the owners. Many of the veterans agreed that we had never before seen the type of drama that Bobby provoked. But we were told that no changes would be made until the end of the year.

As a man who made a living as a hitter, it was hard to watch my team struggle offensively in my absence. I was rehabbing and trying my best to get back and help us. I felt guilty for watching my boys and not being able to pitch in and get it done. They needed me. I was out 35 games and we went 13-22 in that span. I couldn't make it 36 straight games.

I went to Bobby, not the trainers, and told him that I wanted to be out there. I told him that I was no better than 60 percent, and that while I couldn't run the bases, I felt I could jog around them. I knew what the risks were, but I didn't care. I wanted to try. I told Bobby that I wanted to be activated and that he could count on me in the lineup.

Bobby said he appreciated the effort, and he put me in the lineup against Kansas City. My first at-bat I got a hit. My second at-bat I hit a ball to the gap. I was jogging at my 60 percent and watching Jeff Francoeur, who was playing right field. He was a strong-armed outfielder, and I was between first and second. If I continued to jog, he would have me out easily. I sped up in an attempt to reach second quickly, and I felt that same pull that I'd felt a month earlier. I knew then that my season was over, and I thought Bobby understood why. I'd learn later, in a jaw-dropping way, that it was just the opposite.

My season wasn't the only one that was over: the Red Sox careers of González, Beckett, and Crawford were finished the next day. In one of the biggest trades in baseball history, those players and Nick Punto were traded to the Los Angeles Dodgers for role players and prospects. It was the Red Sox's way of saying that they wanted to reset and start over. In any other year, the trade would have blown everyone away in the clubhouse, but people had no idea just how much we had seen since the spring. It made sense that the season would be punctuated in such an unusual way.

I had no guesses about the future and what it held for me. My marriage was dissolving. My team had finished dead last in the division for the first time in 20 years. I was a free agent. And I was hurt. I thought that I would never have to hear from Bobby Valentine again after ownership waited just one day before firing a guy they should never have hired. The biggest surprise to me was not that they hired him. It was that he made it a whole year without someone punching him out.

Of course, Bobby didn't know how to leave town quietly.

I'd heard that he was going to be on TV with Bob Costas, talking about his time in Boston and other things. I was curious. I watched the whole thing and was shocked when I saw him tell Costas that I had quit on him and the Red Sox. All season long, I was the one who had defended him, who had tried to have his back, even when it was an unpopular stance to take as far as my teammates were concerned. But it was the right thing to do, and now he had the balls to go on national TV and suggest that I quit?

I couldn't grab the remote fast enough. I was talking to myself. *This motherfucker* . . . I needed to rewind just to be sure he said what I thought he said. Before I could even rewind, I had reporters texting and calling, asking what I thought of his comments.

Much later, days later, he tried to call me and apologize. I didn't want to hear it. People had called me and warned me about him, but I had tried at every step to prop him up. Then he went on national TV and did that shit to me? That's when you know someone is a bad person. He is a bad person. I don't care what anybody says. That's what I think he is. A bad human being. I'm the one who had his back, out of everybody. And then he said I quit? That was fucked up.

By that time, we had made a trade with Toronto to bring back

John Farrell to be our new manager. I knew him, kind of. Farrell had been our pitching coach when we won the World Series in 2007. I had spent a little time with him, but I didn't know him as well as the pitchers did. This is what I did know: when we traded for him, no one called or texted to say "good luck." I figured we were in good hands.

17

This Is Our F'in City

I looked around our clubhouse, reading the faces of players and staff alike, and noticed something that had not been there in over a year. There was trust in the room. There was peace and respect. There was a new manager who had no interest in making himself the star.

When John Farrell talked with us in Fort Myers for the first time in February 2013, he didn't waste a lot of time recapping the craziness and disappointment of the last-place 2012 season. He made eye contact with some of the players he had won a title with in his first stint with the Red Sox. He looked at me, Dustin Pedroia, Jon Lester, Clay Buchholz, and Jacoby Ellsbury. We had all been there in Denver in October 2007, the night we won the World Series. That was the night we took over the Palm Restaurant, sharing laughs and stories and drinks. The musical group Maroon 5 just happened to be there, and they decided to join us and give an impromptu acoustic performance. That's how a season is supposed to end. Love, fun, music, a raised trophy, and raised glasses.

Farrell wanted to know if that spirit was still in the room in 2013. He had arrived with a reputation as a good and direct communicator, and I could see why. I liked the way he spoke. He never tried to bullshit us. He was a smart man, but not the type trying to prove that he was smarter than you. He was the opposite of Bobby Valentine. He told us that he could sense that we were a hardworking team, and that he had not returned to nitpick and bust balls.

"You guys are adults," he said. "You know what you should and shouldn't be doing. I'm here to be a part of the solution, to get us back to where we belong."

He knew he didn't have to say much more than that. The chemistry that we had was incredible, even before our first full-squad workout. We were the perfect mix of talented, hungry, and a little pissed off. All of us had either been called out, overlooked, or flat-out given up on the previous year.

There was still a backlash against the pitching staff because of chicken, beer, and the September collapse of 2011. Fans were angry with Lester, Buchholz, and Lackey. Ellsbury had been hurt in 2012 after missing most of 2010 with an injury. Some fans were down on Pedroia for being critical of Bobby. Even our new players, guys like Shane Victorino, Mike Napoli, and Jonny Gomes, were undervalued and believed they had something to prove.

For me, the biggest on-field issue was the pain in my right Achilles. The injury I got in July 2012 and reaggravated in August was bad, and it could have been worse if it hadn't been for a man who saved my career. His name was Dan Dyrek, a physical therapist who had worked with Larry Bird when he played for the Celtics. The good news for me was that Dan came to the Dominican in the off-season and educated me about my feet. He told me everything about my Achilles and how I would feel during certain stages of rehab, and gave me exercises I needed to do to get myself back on the field. Dan was so knowledgeable about me that my feet got happy when he was around. Besides God, the person most responsible for preserving my career was Dan.

Unfortunately, I would not be able to play with my teammates until Dan and I felt that my Achilles was completely healed. That meant no opening day, but it did not mean I couldn't hang out with these guys. I wasn't sure how good the team would be, but I knew I had never been a part of something like this. These dudes loved baseball. I had never seen a team that, to a man, sat around and talked about the game so much. One of the cool things they would do was talk about pitching during the game. If one of our hitters got fooled, many players would watch video together to figure out how it happened.

It was a close and passionate team. Funny too. One of the new pitchers was Ryan Dempster, a veteran pitcher who also liked to dabble in stand-up comedy. One of the characters he played for us was a "jock" named Jack Hammer. Dempster would put on his cleats, pull his red baseball socks up to his knees, and wear a jock strap with no pants over it. Then he would give his baseball observations as Mr. Hammer. It was silly, but it was yet another reason for us to hang around the park and talk and laugh together.

I think our identity was set in the first game of the season. Opening at Yankee Stadium, we began the season aggressively. Lester attacked the Yankees with first-pitch strikes, we took extra bases, we showed our toughness by driving in two-out runs, and we were never afraid to celebrate when someone did something — anything, really — positive.

Going into our annual Patriots' Day game on the Monday of the Boston Marathon, we were 7-4. One of the many traditions I looked forward to in Boston was Marathon Monday. It was a Massachusetts holiday, and it often seemed like an all-day party. There was no school for kids, so you'd see families spending time together watching the Marathon. People would do all sorts of generous things for the runners, from holding signs to giving out cups of water to cheering and clapping for those who needed extra motivation. Everything about the day was special, including our game, which always started at 11:00 a.m.

I may not remember the game details of April 15, 2013, but I'll remember the rest of that day as long as I live. We finished a three-game sweep of Tampa just after 2:00. Shortly after the players walked off the field and into the clubhouse, one of the sweetest sights could be seen on the Fenway lawn. The organization allowed parents and their children to leap the gates and run the bases at the park. It was a simple thing, but you could see and feel the joy in those kids, many of them surely pretending that they'd be in the big leagues one day.

My teammates were preparing for a trip to Cleveland to play the Indians, but I wasn't traveling with them. My plan was to stay home and rehab so I could be ready to start my season when the team returned to Fenway four days later. Staying in New England rather than taking that trip to Ohio changed me. Those four days told me a lot about where I lived, and just how deep my connection was to the city that adopted me.

By the time players left the park for the airport, everyone had heard the devastating news. Two bombs had exploded, 12 seconds apart, on Boylston Street, near the Marathon finish line. It was an act of terrorism, and at the time no one had any idea who was responsible for it. The blasts caused some horrific injuries, with hundreds of men, women, and children losing limbs and having shrapnel embedded in their skin. Three people, including an eight-year-old boy, were killed. Some of the sidewalks in the Back Bay were covered with blood. Everyone at the finish line — from doctors to law enforcement officials to everyday citizens — was scrambling to save and protect lives. Some of the people who were in the race ran into stores and grabbed shirts or anything they could use as tourniquets in attempts to help those who were badly bleeding.

Each time I heard a report from the scene, I became sick. And yet I kept listening. I was confused by everything I'd seen and heard. I kept asking myself, *Why would someone do this? What kind of psychopath would do something like this?* The Marathon represents everything good about New England. It's the community coming out for something positive and supporting one another. It's support for some people you know and mostly people you don't know. The more I listened the more obvious it seemed that someone intentionally caused this destruction.

It was hard to think about anything else that night, and the next night too. I remember seeing a picture of Martin Richard, that little eight-year-old boy. In the picture, he's smiling, exposing a missing tooth, and holding a sign that reads, NO MORE HURTING PEOPLE. PEACE. He'd drawn two hearts and a symbol for peace on the sign. I thought of how terrible things must have been for his family. My son was eight too, so the targeted casualties truly hit home for me.

Our organization acted quickly. We put a "617" jersey in the dugout, for the area code of Boston, and we began connecting ourselves to the phrase "Boston Strong." We were determined to reach out to, raise funds for, and inspire individuals and groups affected by the bombing. It was a start, but there was so much work to do. And in the first few days, Monday, Tuesday, and Wednesday, no one knew who was to blame.

That all started to change on Thursday. I was at home watching TV, freaking out and getting angry, just like everyone else in New England. The terrorists had been identified through surveillance video: two brothers, one 19 and the other 26, who had spent many years living on Norfolk Street in Cambridge. I couldn't understand how anyone could do that at the Marathon, especially someone who had grown up two miles away from the finish line.

I spent all day Thursday and Friday overcome with emotion. Maybe I would have still felt things that intensely if I had been in Cleveland with the team, but I doubt it. I did not have the mental escape of doing my job and focusing on something else. No, I was at my house, internalizing the sadness and disbelief of the city. These events were happening in our city, the city that had embraced me, and not that far from where I had worked and lived for the past decade.

On Thursday night, the terrorists killed an MIT police officer on Vassar Street in Cambridge, about a mile and a half from Fenway. They also stole a man's car and held him hostage until he escaped and notified police of the terrorists' plan to go to New York and cause more damage. Early Friday morning, in Watertown, there was a shootout between the terrorists and the police. One of the bombers was killed after the confrontation with police, and one was still at large.

It was Friday morning and I was supposed to be playing my first game of the season that night against the Kansas City Royals. But I didn't want to play. I wanted justice. The only way baseball or anything else could be relevant at that time was if it was attached to a plan to help and heal Boston. If it didn't do that, in my opinion, it didn't matter. I had the TV on all day, hopeful that the region could get some good news after a terrible week. The governor of Massachusetts, Deval Patrick, shut down all public transportation and asked all residents to stay in their houses so officials could have a better chance of catching the terrorist. Our game, thankfully, was canceled. The entire region, and country, turned its attention to catching the bomber. Thank God, on Friday night they arrested him. I was happy to see people lining the streets of Watertown, applauding the officers for their important and heroic work.

On Saturday morning, my body felt fine but my soul was heavy. I thought of all the people who'd just wanted to have a happy day and instead were attacked with crude pressure-cooker bombs, packed with nails and metal. I thought of all the people who'd been frightened by what they'd seen and heard and were afraid to leave the house, afraid to send their kids to school, afraid of living. I thought of being an American citizen first, not just a baseball player, and our responsibility to abide by the rules of the country and to protect it.

I was on edge. I knew that week was going to be with all of us forever. As we prepared for the game, I was asked to say a few words on behalf of the players and the team. It was a special day at Fenway, with many of the heroes of the past week present. These were the people who literally were on the ground, saving lives. They were the spine of the city, with their strength and selflessness. I was proud to wear a white home jersey that day with BOSTON printed in red block letters. I saw my friend Tom Menino there. He was the mayor of Boston, and we had hit it off when I first met him. He had the city in his blood, and when he'd first met me ten years earlier, he could sense that I cared about helping people. Governor Patrick was there as well, along with dozens of officers, EMTs, and Marathon bombing survivors. I wished I could have personally hugged and thanked all of them. I knew I wanted to say something as I held that microphone, but I wasn't sure what it was going to be. I didn't have a script. I just wanted to speak from the heart.

I thought it was important to point out the significance of our jersey, because we were trying to represent and play for the city. This city and state were led by Menino and Patrick, who had empowered law enforcement to do their great work during that week. After that, I said something that I hadn't planned to. It came from the pressure building up that entire week, finally being released. I looked at the sellout crowd, and to their surprise, and mine, I said, "This is our fucking city. And nobody is going to dictate our freedom. Stay strong."

There was applause. Then there was music. It must have taken me a few seconds to realize, as I was walking off the field, that I'd said "fucking." I began thinking, *Oh shit. I think I screwed up.* But when I got close to the police and the mayor, they high-fived me hard. They were excited about what I had just said. You know, when people give a speech like that in front of 30,000 or 40,000 people, they usually write things down ahead of time. They want to make sure they're prepared for what they're going to say. That had never crossed my mind. I'm not sure what I would have done with a written speech. Maybe I could have said it with feeling, without the obscenity, but I believed that true feeling had to be a part of it. I was hurting from the past week, and I know a lot of people must have felt just like me.

To my surprise, I didn't get in trouble for what I said. It was the opposite. What I said became a rallying cry for some people. I had no idea that it would come out exactly like that, but I think it stuck with New Englanders because of what they'd experienced. Every emotion imaginable was felt between Monday and Friday. Finally, on Saturday, we were up and fighting again. That's one of the reasons I fit so well in Boston. That's my personality too. Try to knock me out and it's not going to happen. I'll always take on the fight.

Our team would never be able to take away the pain of the tragedy, but we could honor the city with our play and love for each other. That began in that Saturday game, which we won. It continued into early May. After a win against the Twins on the sixth, our record was 21-11. We were in first place and I was hitting .426.

I didn't think anything of my hot start. It was early in the season, and I knew I wasn't going to finish the year with an average over .400. I was more excited about our team and the characters we had in the clubhouse. I was a fan of everyone in the room and they all knew it, so sometimes I'd walk in and greet everyone with an exaggerated, "You guys are goooood!" Every day there was a different player doing something, big or small, to help us win a ball game. They truly were good players, and they were proof of just how far you can go even when you're counted out.

I wasn't counted out before our game on May 7. I was called a suspect and likely cheater. My hot start prompted a visit from *Boston Globe* columnist Dan Shaughnessy. He questioned me about my hitting, my bat speed, my injuries, my nationality, and said I "fit all the formulas" of a cheater.

"I was just drug-tested two days ago," I told him. "I'll send you the results if you want."

I felt he was asking me certain things because of where I grew up, and he confirmed what I thought when he wrote about Dominicans and performance-enhancing drugs in his column. I thought it was disrespectful and racist. In the column, he wanted to pat himself on the back for asking me the questions in person. I might have been more impressed if he'd called me a cheater to my face instead of being so passive-aggressive.

This was part of playing in Boston that I'd learned to channel into something positive. Keep in mind that Shaughnessy was one of the people who wrote that I was done in 2009 and 2010. He and others believed the *New York Times* report, and they suggested that my success was due to steroids. I wasn't done in 2009. I made the All-Star team in 2010, 2011, and 2012. I got off to a great start in 2013 and now the problem was not that I sucked, but that I was too good? How does that make any sense?

I can understand criticism for not having a good year. It's okay. But you're also going to be critical of a player when he's doing well? That happens in Boston. I haven't seen it happen in New York. Shaughnessy was crushing me, and that motherfucker still walks around like he owns the team. What's the message that's being sent to the rest of the players? *Man, they're crushing David Ortiz . . . crushing the man who runs the show in the clubhouse.* In the long run, it's going to catch up to the organization.

I tried to explain to reporters who asked that I got drug-tested more than anybody by those guys who'd been hired by the MLB owners and the players' association. I was willing to bet that, if they kept records for tests, I held the record. Even the guys who had tested positive for something known didn't get tested as much as I did. It's as if they kept testing me because they were thinking, *We can't believe you're still bangin' after all these years*. They said the tests were random. That's what they said. But I was in there all the time, so either their random machine loved me, or they were lying.

Once, I got a funny story out of a drug test. It was just before the golf classic in the Dominican, and there was a tester who tracked me down there. Well, he almost tracked me down. He called me from the airport and said he was lost. The guy came to test me for PEDs, and he didn't even know where he was going. Crazy. Now, if I had been up to something sinister, I would have told the confused tester to keep driving in circles until he was off the island. Instead, I said, "Where you at? I'll come get you."

In the spring and summer of 2013, I had more serious things to think about than cynics and skeptics. I was 37 years old and thinking about what I was doing with my life. I missed my wife. I missed my kids. I missed being who I was. The kids still came to the games, and I was still involved in their lives, but I missed being a daily presence. We still loved each other, and the time away made me appreciate how powerful our family, at its best, could be. And I was thinking in terms of "our." I'd always felt that way, and it became clearer when my father-in-law, Terry Brick, died that summer. Tiffany was grieving, and so was I. It was becoming a mission season for me: help the city, help the team, help put my family back together again.

I believed in our team as much as anybody, but even I was surprised at times by our collective desire to learn. That stood out for me in late June, when we traveled to Detroit for a four-game series. We felt that we matched up well against the Tigers, despite their roster of stars. We didn't make our case in the series, losing three of four. But our response to a key at-bat let me know that we'd be okay against anyone, especially when the games became more important.

In the final game of the series, a reliever named Joaquín Benoit faced us in the top of the ninth inning. We trailed 7–4, but the heart of the lineup was due. Benoit gave up a single to Pedroia, and I was up next. I knew it was going to be a battle, but I didn't know that he'd perfected a changeup. It was a gem. He threw me that pitch on a 2-2 count and struck me out swinging. We got a run off him in the ninth, but we still lost the game.

Later, the whole team went to the video room and watched that at-bat. I was sitting at the computer and could hear all the voices behind me as Benoit's out pitch was released. "Damn, that was nasty." It was a pitch that started in the strike zone, and once it got to the contact point it dropped. Benoit had a 95-mile-per-hour fastball, but that changeup was like 85, 86. I told my teammates, "The next time I face him, I'm going to look for that pitch the entire at-bat."

We won nine of the next ten games after leaving Detroit, and we led the division by five and a half games. Our lead at the All-Star break was two and a half. I made my fourth consecutive All-Star team and had 19 home runs in mid-July. No matter when the temperature of our team was checked, whether it was Memorial Day, Father's Day, the Fourth of July, or Labor Day, we were the same. Steady. Tough. Resilient.

My favorite statistic about our team was that we made it through the entire regular season without losing three games in a row. The numbers don't always tell the story of what a team is, but that stat does. It's proof that shutting our team down over a long period was almost impossible. Players figured out the flaws on other teams and shared whatever they learned with everyone else. I'm not just talking about starting players; everyone would do that.

One of the players who blew me away was Jonny Gomes. He would prepare for games like a football player. He was always talking about baseball, analyzing what pitchers wanted to do, and thinking about the best ways to attack a weakness. Jonny is one of those players you have to play with to understand his value. I remember thinking that if I were the general manager of the Red Sox, I'd sign Jonny to a five-year contract. The agreement would be that if he couldn't play through that contract, he'd be a part of the organization as a coach or something else. With all the money in the game, it's important to have players like Jonny, players who remind you that what drives everything is a pure love for baseball.

I'd like to think people will say that about our 2013 team. We finished the regular season with 97 wins and the division title. We had gone from last place to first, and we won back many fans who had questioned our commitment to winning in 2011 and 2012. I was excited to be playing again in October rather than looking back and explaining what had gone wrong. We'd been out of the playoffs for four years, and I was more serious about the postseason than at any point in my career. I was a month away from my 38th birthday, and I didn't know how many more playoff opportunities I'd have in my baseball life. I felt fine, but I was realistic. Thirty-eight is not 28. I wasn't going to play much longer.

Our opponent in the first round of the playoffs was Tampa. I respected them, especially their pitching, but I didn't think they had enough offense to beat us in the five-game division series. We had had some tense moments with the Rays over the years. They were one of the lowest-payroll teams in baseball, yet they always seemed to maximize each dollar with smart, low-risk signings. They played with an attitude and edge, and I liked it.

We took care of them in our first game, at Fenway, 12–2. It was a strange game. Our ace, Jon Lester, started for us. He gave up two runs early, and we were being shut down by their starter, Matt Moore. And then the game changed when I came to bat in the fourth, although I didn't do anything unusual. I hit a fly ball to right field that I thought was going to be caught by their right fielder, Wil Myers. He was under the ball, and then he lost it. It bounced into the bullpen for a gift double. That led to a five-run fourth for us, and then we added three more in the fifth to turn a close game into a runaway.

Game 2 went from strange to personal. Their starter was David Price, who our team was introduced to in 2008. He was a rookie reliever then, and he'd closed us out in the American League Championship Series. He was only 28 now, but he'd grown up a lot since then, and had won the Cy Young Award in 2012. He was a tough pitcher for anyone to hit, but devastating on left-handers. He'd given up just two home runs the entire season to those of us on the left side, allowing a .189 batting average. My career numbers against Price were not good: a .216 batting average with no home runs.

I was fortunate against him on that Saturday evening. I connected with a fastball and turned it into a home run, deep into our bullpen, in the first inning. Price was still on the mound in the eighth, even though we led 6–4. I was first up in the inning, and I pulled another fastball deep to right field. It seemed to hug the Pesky Pole for a while, and I stood at the plate watching the ball and the umpire for the fair-or-foul signal. Price didn't like it, and everyone watching on TV could see that. I wouldn't be surprised if a dozen thoughts were flashing through his mind, including the important ones: as the Rays' ace, he hadn't picked them up, and being down to us 0–2 most likely meant their season would be over soon. Complaining about me and my approach to home runs masked the deeper issues.

Long after we won the game, I got a phone call while I was on our team bus. It was Price. I had had small talk with him before and he had always been laid-back and cool. Not this time. He was pissed.

"Man, why'd you embarrass me like that?" he asked.

I didn't agree with the way he was putting it. I told him that I'd never try to embarrass him unless he gave me a reason to. Eventually I said, "Listen, you're a great player. Stop showing people that this stuff bothers you. It makes you look soft."

All the guys on the bus with me were interested in the conversation, especially Jonny, who played with Price in Tampa. Jonny said that Price was one of the best teammates he'd ever had, but his mentality was that no one should be able to get him for two homers in a game like I had.

"He's got to realize that he's dealing with someone of his caliber," Jonny said. "He's not just talking about any hitter. So where is this going?"

To Price's credit, he called back after our initial conversation and apologized. I thought it was over, but learned much later that there was still some resentment. The series was essentially over, though: Tampa won Game 3, but we wrapped it up with a shutdown win in Game 4. We were on our way to the American League Championship Series, prepared to face the talented Tigers.

We had lost our season series to Detroit, and all you had to do was look at the Tigers' rotation to know why. All of their starters were good, from the obvious leaders, Justin Verlander and Max Scherzer, to the more understated Game 1 starter, Aníbal Sánchez. We'd played the Tigers seven times in the regular season and missed Sánchez each time.

Seeing him for the first time in Game 1 made me realize how lucky we had been not to have to face him all season. He had finished as the ERA champion in 2013, giving up only a couple of runs per outing. The way he pitched in Game 1 made me wonder how anyone ever scored against him at all. He seemed to be throwing invisible balls to the plate. We drew six walks off him, but I still think he pitched the game of his life. He didn't give up any hits in six innings and struck out 12. He turned the game over to the bullpen, and they got five more strikeouts against a single hit. That was it. And that hit came in the ninth inning. We were that close to being no-hit to begin a playoff series. Lester had been amazing against them too, allowing a run in six innings. But the talk of the night was their pitching in a 1–0 win.

The next game, through five innings, was more of the same. Scherzer was on the mound, and we didn't have a hit. A normal Scherzer was a dominant pitcher, but this Game 2 version exceeded the standard. He was spotting his fastball better than ever. His velocity was up to 98 at times, and he was throwing the ball where he liked, not where the hitter wanted it. With mastery like that, it's tough to hit a slider and a changeup, and we didn't. We were being no-hit again through five.

People around the game talk, and sometimes you're not sure if what you hear is true or not. I'd heard that Scherzer had said he was going to pitch no more than seven innings or 100 pitches. I wanted that to be true.

We managed to get our first hit earlier than in Game 1. It came in the sixth with a soft liner by Shane Victorino. We pushed across a run as well. I couldn't help us add to it, though, because Scherzer got me to strike out on a slider low in the zone. We had struck out 28 times in the first 15 innings of the series and been outscored 6–1.

One of the quirks about Fenway, and about Boston, is that it doesn't take much there to give people hope. We had appeared to be overmatched in the series, and Fenway was quiet. But when Pedroia doubled off the Monster to drive in our first run, the old park came alive. I'd seen it dozens of times, and it always gave me goosebumps. It was that feeling that a big moment was coming, and I didn't want to be left out. Something was in the New England atmosphere all day. Earlier in the afternoon, the New England Patriots won their game late, with a Tom Brady touchdown pass in the final five seconds. There was something in the air.

I liked our chances to do something because of who wasn't there to begin the eighth. Indeed, Scherzer was out, after striking out 13 and allowing two hits. No one else who came into the game was going to hurt us like Scherzer had. The new pitcher, José Veras, gave up a double to Will Middlebrooks. The crowd sprang to life again, and Tigers manager Jim Leyland wanted no part of it. He quickly got

Veras out of the game and brought in a lefty, Drew Smyly, to pitch to the left-handed Ellsbury. But after Ellsbury walked, putting runners on first and second, Leyland was in action again. Out: Smyly. In: Al Alburquerque. The move seemed to be a good one when Victorino struck out. Then Pedroia singled, my boy Torii Hunter quickly retrieved the ball to hold Middlebrooks at third, and it was time for Leyland to make an important decision.

The bases were loaded with one out in the eighth. I was coming to the plate. Leyland looked to the bullpen and brought in a man I'd been waiting to see for three and a half months: Joaquín Benoit. Swear to God, my first thought when I saw him running in from the bullpen was, *Here comes my changeup.*

I didn't know if he was going to throw it the first pitch, third, or fifth, but I knew I would see it. I tried to think with him. He knew I was a good fastball hitter, so he had to be careful throwing it with the bases loaded. That changeup was too good to ignore, and he had gotten me out with it in June. I'd studied it many times, seeing how it dropped magically at the point of contact. If you weren't expecting it, that changeup was an out pitch for sure. But I was determined to sit on it. Sure enough, he threw it on the first pitch. I put a nice swing on it and sent it flying toward right field.

I saw Torii running hard, looking up, and quickly calculating the mechanics of a dynamic catch. I'd seen him do it dozens of times, in the big leagues as well as the minors. He'd won nine Gold Gloves and earned them all. I wouldn't know until much later that he'd had a decent shot at making the catch. The ball just missed his glove and all three of them, Torii, his glove, and the ball, landed in the Red Sox bullpen.

It was a grand slam to tie the score at 5, and Fenway erupted. Torii and I had grown up together with the Twins, and our families had remained close through the years. I knew what he was capable of and he knew what I could do. If he had caught that ball, we would have been in trouble going to Detroit down 0–2, considering the unbelievable pitching we were facing. He understood how important that home run was to the game and the series. At 38 years old, he was still a damn good outfielder and could run as well as a player ten years younger. He went all out for it, missed it by eight inches to a foot, and I knew then that we would win the series.

Seriously.

We had an opening, and we had taken advantage of every opportunity that had come our way all season. Why would we change now? If we weren't out of the series after those back-to-back starts by Sánchez and Scherzer, nothing was going to stop us. We won Game 2 in the ninth, 6–5. A single run was scored in Game 3, Mike Napoli's home run off Verlander, so we now led a series in which the opponent's starters had allowed a total of two runs in three games. Man, I loved our team. In 2011, on paper, our team wasn't supposed to lose and we couldn't win when it mattered. In 2013, our team wasn't supposed to be shit on paper and we couldn't lose. You can never take the heartbeat and personality out of this game. Never. It makes up for a lot of deficiencies.

We went back and forth with the Tigers in Games 4 and 5, and that put us one win from the pennant. It was as if the series had restarted. We were back at Fenway for Game 6, and the starting pitcher was Scherzer. Although he wasn't as sharp as he'd been in Game 2, he was good enough to be pitching with a 2–1 lead with one out in the seventh. But when he walked our rookie third baseman, Xander Bogaerts, he was taken out of the game.

Bogaerts was on first, Jonny was on second, and Ellsbury was at the plate facing Smyly. In Game 2, Ellsbury had walked in this matchup. In Game 6, he reached on an error by one of our former teammates. José Iglesias had been part of a three-way trade in July between the Tigers, White Sox, and Red Sox. Iglesias was one of the best fielders I had ever seen, surehanded and fluid. The ball from Ellsbury was hit right at him and briefly went into his glove, but he dropped the ball. The bases were loaded for Victorino. It was perfect. Anyone who didn't understand who we were, and what we represented, could have learned in that Victorino at-bat.

It started with Victorino's signing, which had been questioned by many in baseball. He was supposedly a declining player, yet he had given us Gold Glove defense in right field all season. He'd also produced 15 home runs and a career-high .294 batting average. He came to the park every day eager to prove that the scouting report on him was wrong. He was tough. He was positive about our team and angry about any slight against it. That was the snapshot of all of us.

All season he had made pitchers pay for mistakes. In this at-bat, he was facing José Veras, who had a 95-mile-per-hour fastball with good movement. But the first pitch Veras threw was a curveball for a strike. His second pitch was a curveball that Victorino fouled off. Remember, this is a man who can throw the heat. If he had thrown that to Victorino, he probably would have gotten him out. Instead, he threw another breaking ball and Victorino pulled it to the Monster and out of the park. Grand slam, again. He rounded the bases yelling, pounding his chest. We all understood what he was thinking. It was yet another night when someone on our team got payback on somebody who had said they were no good.

We were going to the World Series.

The spring had begun so terribly, with so much sadness in the city. Lives had been lost, and survivors had been changed forever. I had wanted to do my part, and have the team do its part, by bringing smiles to as many faces as possible.

There was no doubt that we were going to beat the St. Louis Cardinals in the Series, and not just because I wanted it to happen. I had a few ideas running through my mind. One was that I never gave them a shot to beat us because I didn't think they were strong offensively.

This is how I looked at it a couple of days before Game 1: whoever hit the best was going to win it because our pitching was about the same.

I also had a maturity and intensity that was more pronounced than it had been six years earlier, the last time I was in the Series. Younger players don't always understand the postseason, and how it's no time to be messing around. I took the playoffs more seriously than anything because I felt it was my time to do something special and get locked in. We owed it to the people of Boston, who had seen such tragedy on their streets that year.

I had looked at some playoff predictions and noticed that the Cardinals were getting a lot of attention for their starting pitching, specifically Adam Wainwright and Michael Wacha. I'd studied their entire staff, starters and relievers alike, and I thought I had a good handle on what they did well. For example, they planned to start Wainwright against us in Game 1, although I believed Wacha's style was much more effective against an American League team. I knew we'd be all right against Wainwright. We put three runs on him in the first inning of Game 1, and two in the second. We also had Jon Lester pitching, so it was an easy night for us. We won 8–1.

Game 2, also at Fenway, was interesting. It was the first time we had faced the rookie Wacha, and I knew what my guys were going through during the game. He was mowing us down, but we were quickly getting a feel for what he liked to do. I knew if it turned into a long Series and we saw Wacha again, he would not have the success he had in Game 2. In fact, I talked about that *during* Game 2.

In my first at-bat against him, I grounded out. I walked my second time up. Before my third at-bat, I told one of our pitchers, Jake Peavy, that I was comfortable with my scouting report: Wacha had a good fastball and he liked it, but he really loved his changeup. He'd throw it at any time. It was his best pitch. I told Peavy, "He's going to keep leaving that thing up, and I'm gonna hit it out. Opposite field."

That's what happened in the sixth, and it gave us a 2–1 lead. When I got back to the dugout, Peavy kept looking at me and shaking his head. "What the hell?" he said. "You called it and did it, like you've done it before."

It wasn't a mystery. Just homework. It was why I spent so much time, in and out of season, thinking and dreaming about the habits of pitchers. That was the payoff. Peavy must have talked to me for a week about calling that home run.

The Cardinals came back to win Game 2, and they went back to St. Louis to win Game 3 as well. In the middle of Game 4, with the score tied at 1, I decided to say something to the team in the dugout. We were down 2–1 in the Series, and we were playing like zombies. Quiet, no emotion, a little stiff.

I gathered my boys around and wanted to drop some knowledge.

"You think you're going to come to the World Series every year?" I said. "It's not gonna happen. You don't come to this every year. So do you know what you do when you come to this? You give everything you have, as if it's your last ride. You don't let the opposition fuck you up just because you're scared and you're panicking."

I told them that we were better than the Cardinals, and better than we'd played so far. Then I asked a question that I already knew the answer to: "Are you scared? Who's scared here?" Nobody raised a hand. After that, it was time for the conclusion: "Then let's fucking go."

In the sixth inning, we woke up and never looked back for the rest of the Series. Pedroia singled, and I followed him with a walk. That set the stage for Jonny, who I was honored to call a teammate. He was always ready to put in work, no matter what the situation. He was a late addition to the lineup, and he made John Farrell look smart. Jonny's three-run homer gave us the lead and the eventual win. The Series was tied at 2, and we had a couple of things going in our favor.

One was that I was locked in and the Cardinals continued to pitch to me. And I knew the reason. Their manager, Mike Matheny, was a former catcher. And catchers, in their minds, think they can get a motherfucker out. Anytime. They don't understand that when a motherfucker is hot, he's hot. Then the whole team gets hot. That's how it works, and that's eventually what happened to us in Game 6.

But before we got there, we had the other factor that worked to our advantage. Lester. He had been the best pitcher of the postseason, and that didn't change in Game 5. He was on fire again, allowing one run and four hits in a 3–1 win. We'd gone to St. Louis down 2–1, and after winning two out of three, we were in position to clinch the World Series in front of fans who'd been through hell in 2013. They deserved it. The pitcher standing between us and clinching was the rookie Michael Wacha.

We were ready for him. All of us. The Cardinals walked me four times in the game, but it was too late to be cautious. Our team was relaxed, so much so that before the game we sat around being entertained by the shirtless, jock-strap-wearing, high-socks-sporting Jack Hammer. I knew then that we were going to win the Series that night. I had hit .688 in the Series and would be named Most Valuable Player. Everyone commented on how I would come through, again, in the clutch.

My wife saw it differently. She told me something that I would never forget. She said, "As clutch as you were on the field, you did that and more to win me back and put our family back together." Let me tell you, it was a miracle. I had been separated from my wife for a year, and I was an autograph away from being divorced. And it didn't happen. That's not how those stories usually end.

The final act of our season was just as poetic. We paraded through the city, waving to millions of Red Sox fans who had fallen in love with our team again after some hard times. When we got to Boylston Street, near the Marathon finish line, we stopped and sang "God Bless America." I'd met some of the survivors throughout the summer and seen up close how their lives had been altered forever. And that was just what I could see. No one could be the same after experiencing that in their city. We'd all been changed somehow.

Winning the World Series helped a lot of people get closer to the normal they once knew. I was proud of that, and even more proud of the way we'd been able to celebrate as a region. With millions of people coming together in downtown Boston, there were just a few arrests and no disturbing incidents. Despite what happened in April, we had defended and retained our freedom.

I'm telling you, as I look back on the year and realize how everything ended up, all I can say is that God is great. God is great because we went from a storm to a day like the parade. It went from the worst it could be to the best it could be. A recovery takes a while, and our city did it in the same year as the tragedy.

A lot of things went through my head at the finish line, but I kept coming back to the miraculous nature of it all. I couldn't believe how far we'd come.

18

Ups, Downs, Silver Linings

John Henry may have done it for a variety of reasons. Maybe it was because he'd watched me hit .688 in the World Series and take home the Series MVP award. It could have been connected to the plaque he gave me years earlier, a plaque that remains in my house to this day: most clutch player in team history.

I didn't know the specific reason the Red Sox owner personally decided to close the deal on my contract extension, but I was relieved that he did.

"We're going to give you a contract that allows you to play as long as you want to," he told me in the spring of 2014. "We want you to end your career with the Red Sox."

It wasn't the money itself that provided the relief. It was the owner saying he cared and then doing something to show it. It was the fact that I didn't have to talk about it anymore. The media portrayals had some fans believing that I liked the topic, or that I was simply greedy. That wasn't the case. I was thankful that Mr. Henry removed a story line that should not have been there in the first place.

I never understood why I had to fight Red Sox general managers so hard to get what I deserved. As much credit as Theo Epstein got for signing me back in 2003, I don't think he ever fully appreciated who

I was. He would make me sweat out my deals and then turn around and give out some of the worst long-term contracts in baseball. The numbers were always going up: $39 million for Julio Lugo . . . $40 million for Edgar Rentería . . . $70 million for J. D. Drew . . . over $100 million to bid on and sign Daisuke Matsuzaka . . . over $140 million to sign Carl Crawford. When Theo left after the 2011 season and Ben Cherington took over, one of the first things Ben did was take me to the brink of arbitration. Think about that for a second. I was the guy in the middle of the lineup hitting 30 home runs and getting 100 runs batted in, year after year after year. Why would you ever have contract issues with that guy? I'm your "franchise player." I am not asking you to give me something that I haven't earned. For example, in 2011 I'd hit 29 home runs and 40 doubles, and yet I was steps away from arbitration. In the final hour, literally, we agreed on a one-year deal.

I thought it was bullshit, all of it: the fact that I was putting dollars in pockets, yet had to beg for my cut; the fact that money flowed freely to players who hadn't played a day in Boston; the fact that my contract was never resolved smoothly and privately, so I could put my focus elsewhere.

That's why I thought Mr. Henry's move was so wise. It allowed me to put my mind fully on training and preparing for 2014. I knew I didn't have many seasons left in my career, and I wanted to do everything possible to win another championship. But while I may have had Mr. Henry's ear on financial matters, I couldn't seem to capture Cherington's when it came to personnel.

I tried to give Ben advice one time, and he didn't listen. Nelson Cruz was coming off a 50-game suspension for performance-enhancing drugs, but he was available. Because of the suspension, I thought he was a low-risk signing that could help us. He was a big-hitting left fielder who was facing a public relations problem. That was exactly the reason he might have been available for short money. I don't know if it was the suspension that scared Ben, or if he just didn't like the player. I liked Cruz personally, and I believed that any problems he had in the past were behind him. That didn't seem to matter to Ben, because talking to him about Cruz was like talking to the wall.

At 38 years old, I thought about team-building like never before. I had urgency. For most of my career, it hadn't been my style to go to general managers and get into their shit. I was content to go about my business. But I was hungry to win as much as I could before I left the game. I was no front-office expert, but I did know a few things: Boston, good baseball players, and what we needed. I told Ben that Cruz would be perfect for our team and the city as well. Some players don't have the toughness and thick skin necessary to play in Boston, but Cruz did. If he was slotted behind me in the lineup, we could do some damage.

That was the extent of it for me. Some players will get a GM's ear and wear him out with opinions and observations. I'm not that kind of person. I'll tell you the things that I think we need, and then leave it up to you to sign him or not. I'm not going to be busting your balls. We didn't sign Cruz and he went to Baltimore, in our division, instead. I thought he was a great fit for the Orioles.

Our biggest issue, even as early as spring training, was much more serious than not having Cruz. And I admit, I was shocked by it.

Spring workouts began just four months after the World Series. Anyone who had watched the Series, and the entire playoffs, could see that Jon Lester was better than anyone else when the games were most important. He'd been great for us in each series, against three teams — the Rays, Tigers, and Cardinals — with varying styles and talent levels. He was our best starter, and we needed him. He was also in his contract year, and the Red Sox repeated an error that had been driving me crazy for years. They offered Lester a salary lower than he was worth, and you just knew that sometime soon they were going to pay an unknown player much more than his worth.

It was frustrating.

I heard a lot of talk about salaries in baseball, and how the Red Sox were not going to extend long contracts to pitchers over 30. Lester had just turned 30. I also think some people had gotten the wrong idea about how we won in 2013. We got a lot of attention for our chemistry and for signing players such as Mike Napoli, Shane Victorino, and Ryan Dempster to reasonable, short-term contracts. That was true, but we didn't win the Series solely because of those contracts. We had a good mix of role players and stars, and it wasn't a bad thing to have hardworking stars signed long-term.

I didn't know what the Red Sox were thinking, but I didn't like it. Max Scherzer was a great pitcher for the Tigers, and he was in his contract year like Lester was. Detroit tried to convince him to sign before free agency by offering him $24 million per season over six years. Boston offered Lester $17 million per season over four years. Yes, both salaries are huge when compared to the wages earned by hardworking people who are not professional athletes. In our industry, though, Scherzer's offer was competitive and Lester's was below market.

My deal was taken care of, and I was pleased about that. But I knew we were in trouble if we were going to maintain that stance on Lester. I had a bad feeling about us, on the field and off. How could anyone in management offer Lester that when the market called for something so much higher? What they were basically telling him was to go fuck himself.

The tone and feel of camp, players versus management, was already different than it was in 2013, and we hadn't played a game yet. It was going to get worse, quicker than any of us expected. But before that happened, there were some light moments off the field that reminded me just how long and pleasant my baseball journey had been.

One Saturday evening, I got a call from a friend of mine who excitedly broke the news.

"Honestly, I know you've really made it now, brother!" he said.

I asked him what he was talking about.

"You've made it to *Saturday Night Live* . . . someone is doing *you* on *Saturday Night Live*. You've made it now, brother!"

I didn't see what he was describing until later, and it made me smile. In this *SNL* skit, the actor Kenan Thompson was pretending to be Big Papi. What made it funny was that he exaggerated everything about me: the beard, the accent, the things I like to talk about. He spent a lot of time talking about popular Dominican foods like *sancocho, pollo guisado,* and what appeared to be his favorite thing to say, *mofongo Dominicano*. My opinion about things like that is they should make you happy. And a skit like that promotes your image when no one is saying anything bad about you.

The public that watches *Saturday Night Live* isn't 100 percent the same as the one that watches baseball. Now you're getting a new audience that may not know anything about baseball, Big Papi, or even the Dominican Republic. You never know what that might inspire people to do. Research the food that Kenan was talking about? Find out about the Dominican? Maybe even learn more about me and what I went through to get to the majors?

That's why I never looked at the skit as a negative, even though I know some people did. They thought it reinforced Latin American stereotypes. I thought it was comical while being potentially educational, so I was flattered by it.

Winning the World Series didn't just lead to material for comics in New York. It brought me and my teammates to the White House to meet with President Barack Obama. I already had a lot of respect for him for the way he'd handled the recovery from the bombing at the Marathon. He gave an incredibly inspiring speech in which he said that Boston would run again and win again. He'd even mentioned the sports teams having another parade down Boylston Street. He'd said that in April 2013. We'd won in October 2013. In April 2014, we were in Washington on the South Lawn, listening to him give a speech about our team.

I held an Obama Red Sox jersey, number 44, for the president. After he had spoken for about ten minutes, I handed him the jersey and then made a request. I brought out my cell phone and asked for a selfie. It was one of the best pictures I've ever taken, and people on social media agreed with me: within an hour or two, the image had been retweeted more than 40,000 times.

As someone who wasn't born in the United States, it was an honor for me to stand there as an American citizen. I think Obama is the coolest president the United States will ever have. Total calm and cool. When he was walking toward me, I thought, *As an American, you have to be proud to have a cool-ass president like this one.*

When our World Series honeymoon and tributes wore off after a couple of months, it was easy to see our weaknesses. Our run production evaporated. We'd lost our leadoff hitter, Jacoby Ellsbury, to the Yankees. Our number-two hitter in 2013, Shane Victorino, was fighting injuries. The three and four hitters, Pedroia and I, had good numbers. They just weren't numbers that put us on a pace similar to the championship season. Mike Napoli was the number-five hitter, but he'd also dipped from 2013. Xander Bogaerts was expected to make the leap from effective contributor to reliable starter, but his adjustment period was longer and rougher than predicted. We struggled in center with Ellsbury's departure.

We were sliding. We were a back-and-forth team in April. We were slightly below average in May and early June. By the time we got to July and the All-Star break, we were just bad. We were in last place and Baltimore was in first. The Orioles had many good things going for them, and one of them was Nelson Cruz being selected to play in the All-Star Game.

In our previous disappointing season, 2012, we had made a big trade that signaled a new direction for the franchise. The same thing happened at the deadline in 2014. I couldn't believe we'd changed so quickly. I felt like I could still hear the cheers on Boylston Street. I could still remember the faces, the smiles, the excitement of the fans waving at us as the Duck Boats passed by.

It seemed that it was being taken away, significant piece by significant piece. It was hard. Not only were these my boys, they were also good. I remember once teasing Chris Davis from Baltimore about Andrew Miller. Miller was our six-foot-seven left-handed reliever, and he used to make Davis look like shit. Davis is a friend of mine, so I got to first base and said, "My man, that guy is filthy, isn't he?"

Davis gave the most honest and real answer: "I don't know what to do against him. It's like he knows what you're thinking. He doesn't give you shit to hit." He was right. The next day Davis was facing Miller, and he threw a slider so nasty that it almost went into our dugout. I was laughing my ass off.

It was no time for laughing when Miller was traded to the Orioles for a pitching prospect named Eduardo Rodríguez. I immediately thought of Davis laughing at me now. It was going to be my turn to deal with Miller as an opponent.

We also traded John Lackey, who pitched with a lot of toughness and attitude. He knew what he was doing on the mound. Even when he didn't have his best stuff, he gave his team a chance to win. He was moved to the Cardinals for a hitter named Allen Craig and pitcher Joe Kelly.

The big move, though, was Lester. He was one of my brothers. I respected him and trusted him in big situations. No one could say anything about his resolve, in baseball or in life. He'd beaten cancer as a young pitcher and then returned to win the clinching game of the 2007 World Series. He'd been unhittable at times in 2013. He'd seen a lot of the same things in Boston that I had, experienced some of the same bullshit from the media and the team, yet he still wanted to be a part of the Red Sox. He was like me in that he had the city and the organization in his blood. At times, it seemed that when the Red Sox knew that about you, they'd try to take advantage with some "hometown discount" that didn't measure up to what you deserved.

Lester and the Red Sox couldn't figure out a deal, so they traded him to the A's for an outfielder named Yoenis Céspedes. To make things worse, it wasn't just Lester being traded to Oakland. Jonny Gomes, one of the best teammates I've ever had, was sent there with him.

The season was no longer about winning. It was about development. And that's tough to hear in early August, especially when you're 38 and trying to maximize your remaining years. I could understand the value of picking up prospects, but not at the expense of winning. I knew the Red Sox had money, and they were one of the teams that could keep veterans and go all out for young players. Our championship teams always had a blend of both.

Three weeks after trading Lester, the team opened up its checkbook and gave $72.5 million to a 27-year-old Cuban outfielder named Rusney Castillo. Now, I know they would just call it the price of doing business, but they never seemed to get how stupid these moves looked to veteran players. I had nothing against Rusney. The concern was that over $70 million could be given to someone who hadn't spent a day in the majors and had not been actively playing baseball for a year. Meanwhile, they had just traded away one of the best big-game pitchers, a pitcher the Red Sox developed, all because they didn't want to pay him what he deserved.

I couldn't figure it out when the signing happened in August, and I didn't have better answers when the season ended in October. We had lost 91 games, two fewer losses than we had had in 2012. Two last-place finishes surrounding a World Series title. It was weird. Maybe stranger than that was how we couldn't score runs anymore. A team like Tampa, for example, always had to hunt for runs. They'd finished 2014 as the worst run-scoring team in the American League. We'd scored just 22 more runs than they had all season. Baltimore finished ahead of us by 25 games, and to this day I think that if we'd gotten Cruz instead of the Orioles, we would have made the playoffs.

Our year, on the field and philosophically, was bad.

Then, in free agency, things got even stranger. The Red Sox wanted to improve the lineup, understandably, so Pablo Sandoval and Hanley Ramírez were targets. Hanley always told me that he looked up to me, and I knew I could help make his transition to Boston a smooth one. Pablo, or Panda, was a good man who could bring a lot of talent and personality to our team. There was also a free agent pitcher they wanted, and they were willing to pay well over $100 million to get him.

It was Jon Lester.

We probably could have had him, without negotiations from other teams, for $120 million in the spring. But after becoming a free agent in the fall, he was being chased by the Red Sox, Giants, and Cubs. All high-payroll teams. The number was going to be much higher than $120 million, especially since Theo Epstein was involved. He knew what Lester could bring to a team.

Let me tell you what a special human being Lester is. Even after all the tricks of negotiating, even after being traded by the Red Sox and shown more respect by other teams, he wanted to be here. He called me, crying, because he wanted to come back to the Red Sox. He was bawling, and it got me a little choked up too. I told him that he was a great pitcher and that he shouldn't feel any guilt, because the Red Sox had had the opportunity to prevent free agency from happening.

"Look at your next move this way," I told him. "It's going to be for your family before it's for you. That's a big contract that can set people up for a long time. Go get it."

Theo knew what he was getting in Lester: a good teammate, a good pitcher, a guy who was all about business. I have never seen anyone work harder than that kid. Good players who not only perform at the highest level but can do it in Boston are worth keeping. It's as simple as that. I don't care who's in charge of the Red Sox. If they ask me the key to holding on to talent, I will tell them to find the players who can perform in Boston and keep them.

Going into the 2015 season, I'd been a part of the Red Sox for a dozen years. I'd seen players panic. I'd seen players get scared. I'd seen players wanting to go home. I'd seen players fake injuries. I'd seen all kinds of shit, but none of it ever came from the guys who understood Boston and had figured out how to lock in and perform as a member of the Red Sox.

I'd been fortunate to be a part of a city with a makeup so much like my own. It's funny how things work out. When I was in Minnesota, I had no idea that Boston was where I should have been all along. You get released and it's embarrassing. It makes you unsure of what's coming next, which can be an uncomfortable feeling. Yet, as I looked ahead at 2015, a huge milestone was before me. Five hundred home runs. And I had a chance to do that as a member of the Red Sox.

I was 39 when the season started. I knew I was still a good player, but I wasn't the same as I'd been my first four or five years with the Red Sox. Anybody who really knew baseball and hitting could see the difference. Back in the day, when I hit the ball, it was going in the stands. Now, the balls that used to go in the stands still went there sometimes but many of them scraped the wall or wound up as doubles to the gap. I felt that my knowledge of pitchers was better at 39 than it had been at 29, but strength is strength. You're not going to out-think Father Time.

My love for the game was still there in 2015, despite our team not being much better than the year before. We were better at the plate and worse as a pitching staff. I didn't know who made the call to move on from Lester, and to a degree Lackey, but I thought many times that our season reflected that decision.

The American League East is no joke — it has some of the most elite hitters in baseball. I was always nervous for pitchers who came from another division, like the National League Central, and thought they could get away with the same pitches here. It doesn't work. Also, in this division, you need an ace. There's no way around it. You've got to get him and you've got to pay him.

We had traded Yoenis Céspedes to Detroit for pitcher Rick Porcello, who was 26. I liked Porcello. He had good control and kept the ball on the ground. I thought we needed more pitching, and the stats agreed. On July 1, our team earned run average was at the bottom of the league.

I felt fine physically, although my batting average was just .228. I did have 13 home runs, 21 away from 500 in my career. I've never taken my achievements for granted, but I never played for them either. I'd be lying if I told you that I spent a lot of time thinking about 500 home runs and whether it was going to happen in 2015. I wanted to help us win, but the year was harder than I'd thought it would be.

At times, honestly, I felt old. It took me longer to get ready for games. I required more treatment. I still lifted as much as my teammates, if not more. It just took longer to recover. People at the park would ask how I was doing and I'd tell them one of two things: Papi is old . . . Papi is tired.

The good part of not being a 2015 All-Star was that I could rest. I needed it. I was a different hitter after the break and had 21 home runs going into August, 13 short of 500. That was a milestone that only 26 other players in history had reached. Our organization was changing as well. When you spend a lot of money on a team and it doesn't perform to expectations, there's no patience for that in big markets. Ben Cherington, who had built a championship team two years earlier, was essentially demoted, without losing his job, when the Red Sox hired Dave Dombrowski as president of baseball operations. Dombrowski had worked for John Henry in Florida, and he had recently been the top baseball executive in Detroit. I knew people who'd worked for him, and I'd heard that he was a very involved boss. You were always aware of him. Maybe Ben heard that as well, because he decided to resign rather than stay on board and be the number two to Dombrowski.

It was difficult to think about the pursuit of 500 home runs when much more important things were happening with our team. I liked our manager, John Farrell, a great deal. I felt that his ability to communicate was his strongest asset, and that's important when dealing with a bunch of proud athletes who all want to play. John was strong and proud himself, so he tried to put the team's needs above his own when he managed in pain and didn't tell many people.

I didn't know what to expect that Friday afternoon at Fenway when he gathered us all together for a team meeting. I tried to guess what it was about. We were in last place, which was disappointing, but it wasn't news. We'd struggled all year. But then I looked at John's face, and I could see that something serious had happened. He's a big man, about six-foot-four, with a strong baritone. But he almost seemed to whisper when he told us what was going on. He'd learned, during a procedure to correct a hernia, that he had cancer. Stage 1 lymphoma. He said he was going to take the rest of the season off to focus on his health.

It was silent in the room, and no one had the perfect words. We hugged him and told him that we were going to support him and pray for him. There aren't a lot of people who could have handled things like John did. He'd managed a game, in Miami, knowing that he had been diagnosed with cancer.

The news about John changed my outlook for the rest of the season. Of course, I wanted to have fun and win games. I also forced myself to pause the first two weeks of September as I approached my 500th home run. It wasn't just about the stats. It was a life lesson, a bunch of them. I can't say there was a lesson for each home run, but it was hard for me to put the journey into a neat sentence or two. I thought about so many things. Like sharing. I didn't know when my time in the game would be up, but I knew I wanted to share everything I knew with as many players as possible. My experience with the negativity of some people in baseball inspired me to reach out to players — whether on my team or another team — when I sensed that they were struggling.

I could feel a lot of my bitterness over how I was treated in 2010 turning into something more positive. My experiences had produced an upbeat story for me to tell. On the day I was pinch-hit for in Toronto, my career home run total stood at 318. How many people that day thought that I'd even reach 350? And those who thought I'd get that far probably guessed it would be with another team. It was a lesson to never count myself out. It was a lesson to not count anyone else out either.

There were some unlikely stories in the 500–home run club, but many of those players were anointed as stars when they were teenagers. Mickey Mantle and Ken Griffey Jr., Reggie Jackson and Barry Bonds. Ted Williams and Alex Rodriguez. The scouts saw them coming and cleared the path. My road had been unusual and unexpected. Discovered in the Dominican, released in Minnesota, rescued in Boston, disrespected in Canada, revived again in New England.

I knew that number 500 was going to be special, and not just because it would remind me of crisscrossing the baseball map. I always pointed to heaven after home runs, sharing those moments with my mother. She had loved being the mother of a professional athlete. I loved the thought of her smiling above as her son became a member of even more exclusive company. It finally happened on September 12.

We were in Tampa, where the Rays, like us, were winding down a disappointing season. There were about 20,000 fans in the stands, and many of them made it clear why they were there. Every time I stepped to the plate there would be a commotion and several thousand cell phones flashing. I didn't take the moment for granted, but I wanted it to be over. In the fifth inning, with us already ahead 7–0, I got my kind of pitch from starter Matt Moore. It was low and inside, and I did what I had done 499 other times in my career. I hit it and sent it flying, deep into the stands. I tried not to smile as I circled the bases, but it was hard. I could see both teams standing and clapping outside of their dugouts, and there were even people in the stands who wrote later that they'd come all the way from Haina to see number 500.

My teammates were great. They were as happy for me as they would have been for themselves. I got so many kind words from them, and from other players too. In fact, my cell phone nearly gave out from all the congratulatory texts I received. By the time the game was over, I had at least 75 texts.

I'm not usually in the moment like that, but this was a time to think about life and special occasions. Life changes quickly. John was a perfect example of that. He told me that he was feeling no pain at all before his diagnosis, and then one day he had cancer.

I wanted to be in the mind-set of appreciating everything I had, whether it was my health or the ability to hit 500 home runs in a career. I'd heard about so many great players in baseball history, so many bad boys I'd grown up admiring. When I hit that home run in Tampa off Matt Moore, I thought about what it meant as I ran the bases. One day I was going to be one of those players the scouts talked about. They had said that I was going to be the next Fred Mc-

Griff, and now they'd look at the swing of some 15- or 16-year-old kid and say he's going to be the next David Ortiz.

I was fortunate to finish the season strong after another slow start. I was still getting it done, at 39, with 37 doubles and 37 home runs. Just before my 40th birthday, I got a surprise phone call. It was Dave Dombrowski. He was very respectful, and he wanted to know my opinion about signing a player I'd clashed with in the past — David Price.

Price had complained about me watching my home run in a play-off game. The next year he'd hit me, on purpose, to retaliate. But he was a great pitcher and I wanted to win.

"Don't worry about me and David, we'll be fine," I told Dombrowski.

Besides, I didn't want to get in the way of a long-term signing for the franchise. Price or any other free agent was going to have anywhere from three to seven years with the Red Sox. I hadn't announced it yet, but I was pretty sure that my next season was going to be my last one.

19

The End and a New Beginning

It was a gray Monday morning, April 11, 2016, and I had been awake for a while. Soon I would be in the car, for my 25-minute commute to work. I had been doing some version of this in the big leagues, getting ready for the home opener, since I was 21 years old. Now, at 40, I was preparing for the final season of my career.

Other than the film crew set up in my driveway, there didn't appear to be anything unusual about the day. My family was holding on to a secret that would have me in tears in a few hours, but I was too focused on the game ahead to figure out the plans my wife and children had made with the Red Sox to commemorate my last home opener.

As I made the familiar drive, from suburban back roads to the Massachusetts Turnpike, from the Pike to Fenway, I saw the people who had inspired me for each of the last 14 seasons in Boston. A few blocks away from the park, I could already see hundreds of fans in their Red Sox jerseys and hats, anticipating the opener. I was going to miss this atmosphere, which I truly believe helped shape me as a player and as a person.

I had carried this baseball culture, and this organization, in my blood. It was why I wanted to do everything possible to win ball games. My family had watched me through the years, so they knew about the sacrifices. They understood how much sleep I had lost, how many grade school concerts I had missed, how many practices and lessons I hadn't driven to or even attended. The specialists and some of my teammates knew what I'd done privately. They realized that I'd played in pain, physical and emotional. I'd played as I went through stressful situations and family issues. I had never brought it to the field. I had left it in the Fenway parking lot, at the corner of Yawkey and Van Ness. The show had always gone on.

It wasn't going to be like that much longer. I'd already been warned by Pedro Martínez about what he felt was the biggest adjustment you have to make in retirement. He said it would be the lack of a routine. We had lived with tight schedules since we were teenagers in the minors, always needing to be in a certain place at a certain time. When baseball goes away, a player is suddenly an ex-player with an open schedule. And when the kids are in school, there's the quiet of an empty house. Pedro said it might be uncomfortable at first. He said he missed the field, the competition, and the challenges.

I didn't know what it would be for me, but I knew I wouldn't figure it out for a while. With one more year to play, I wanted to make this one of the best I had ever had.

If the home opener was any indication of what the season would be, I wasn't going to be able to put my head down and think solely of the game. There was going to be a lot of nostalgia from other teams, and even my own. It started a few minutes before the game, and I should have seen it coming. Before I left the house, Tiffany mentioned that the team hadn't planned anything special for my final opener. Then she smiled. I should have known.

As I stood on the field, broadcaster Joe Castiglione introduced the National Anthem singer. He said she had been just two years old when she moved from Minnesota to Boston, due to her father's job. It didn't occur to me, immediately, that he was talking about my

15-year-old daughter Alex. My hat was already off when I saw her, and it was a good thing because I needed something to cover my face as I cried.

She sang the anthem beautifully, which was not a surprise. She's a great singer, and she'd been practicing for her opening day assignment for weeks. We'd come a long way since our first home opener in Boston in 2003. I didn't think then that one day I'd be given a special tribute by the Red Sox, one that would include Bill Russell, Jason Varitek, Ty Law, Pedro, Bobby Orr, Tim Wakefield . . . and the singing of my daughter. I had known back in '03 that I could play, but I hadn't guessed that I would be able to retire on my own terms and be considered the greatest designated hitter of all time. When Alex finished, I composed myself long enough to tell her how much love and pride I had for her.

I had trained hard and well for this last year, so no matter how many obligations and requests I got, I knew the season wasn't just about that. There would be signings, interviews, and commercials. I wasn't going to complain about any of it, because when Alex was that two-year-old girl running around in Pedro's basement, none of those opportunities were available to us. They became a reality because of where we lived, how I performed, and how much the team won. I was determined to give the people of Boston a winning performance one more time.

That April day I knew early that, individually and collectively, we were on to something. I thought our roster was one of the most talented and athletic I'd seen in years. I loved the energy and abilities of young players like Mookie Betts, Xander Bogaerts, and Jackie Bradley Jr. They always asked questions about the back-and-forth adjustments of hitters and pitchers, so I'd begun doing for them what Pedro and Manny had done for me. There was a psychology to each at-bat, a game plan, and as a hitter you couldn't expect to be successful going to the plate with an empty head.

For example, I wanted the young players to see the repeating patterns in how most pitchers dealt with me. I could have taught a whole class on it based just on the way Ubaldo Jiménez pitched to me two days after the opener. Going into the game, my guess was that Ubaldo was going to pitch away and try to force me to get myself out. So I had to go to the plate mindful of that possibility: *Be patient. He's just trying to get you to chase. I've gotten myself out against him because I swung at bad pitches.*

Sure enough, I walked in my first at-bat. I walked in my second at-bat. In my third at-bat, he threw a fastball for a ball and then a splitter for a strike. Now I'm sitting on bullshit. Got it: there was a breaking ball to the back of my leg. Finally, I swung and grounded out to first. It was an out, but I knew what he wanted to do. And once you know what a pitcher wants to do, the chances of success go way up.

For my walk in the third inning, Ubaldo had thrown a slider on a 3-0 count. It was his go-fuck-yourself pitch. Nobody in the league is hitting a 3-0 slider. It was like an intentional walk. As I told my young teammates, it's a hard game that gets a little easier when you have a good idea of the strike zone and how pitchers think. That 3-0 slider? You just can't swing at that. You could bring a random fan out of the stands and he wouldn't swing at that either.

I wanted them to see the effect of a scouting report. It's why everybody pitched me the same way. Everybody. The first pitch was going to be on the outside part of the plate. They never tried to sneak one by me, and they never tried to throw me in. When they came into me, it was a mistake. They didn't try to challenge me. The day after the opener, Mike Wright tried to do that, and I hit that shit into the bullpen. That was my strength, and pitchers knew it. An inside fastball was mine, not theirs. It didn't matter how hard they threw. That's what came naturally to me. That was my strength.

When I took batting practice in the cage, I'd practice hitting the ball to the opposite field. I'm a pure pull hitter, so I worked on hitting the ball off the Green Monster because I knew most pitchers were trying to operate on the outside and those were the most likely pitches I'd get. If my teammates saw me hitting a bunch of doubles off the Monster, they might be like, *Man. This guy is locked in.* But it wasn't really that. I explained to them that I didn't worry about both sides of the plate. If there was one player in the league who didn't have to worry about both sides of the plate, it was me.

I knew the young players would figure it out and get into a routine that worked for them. Their talent is exceptional. I'm amazed by Betts. He asks a ton of questions and walks around, unassuming, with a smile on his face. Then he plays the game and he's a beast. He has everything: smarts, speed, power, character. And he was doing all of that at 23. I didn't figure out half of the stuff I know until I was 27 or 28.

That's something I noticed about our young players as well as players on other teams. They're figuring things out faster than my generation did. Mike Trout was an incredible hitter in his early twenties. Same for Bryce Harper. It's not normal for players to be MVPs that early in their careers. It was fun to watch them go to the plate with confidence because it reminded me of what I used to be able to do. I was still a good player at 40, and I knew it. But at 30, I'd felt that I could do anything I wanted. Look at it this way. One time Russell Martin asked me during the 2016 season, "Papi, why are you so good?" I told him, "Bruh, I used to be better than this." He looked at me like that was impossible. But it was true. I'll bet you a guy like Albert Pujols, who's going to the Hall of Fame, knows what I'm talking about. You go from untouchable greatness to pretty good. You feel the drop-off. It happens to everybody, no matter how good you are.

Our season was developing exactly how I wanted. I knew there would be final-season tributes and interviews along the way. I knew that some of the sponsors I worked with, from JetBlue to Xfinity to Dunkin' Donuts, wanted to do commercials during the year. My hope had been to have those things happen on the perimeter while the focus, mine and everyone else's, remained on the field.

We were doing exactly that at the end of May. After a win in Baltimore, we were 32-20 and in first place in the division. We were murdering pitching. Mookie, who was just starting to warm up, had a three-homer game against the Orioles. He was our leadoff man, but I looked at the way he handled the bat, quick wrists and a powerful swing, and I didn't think he would be out of place in the middle of the order. I was hitting .335 with a slugging percentage of .716. Xander and Jackie were well over .300, at .350 and .331.

I wasn't surprised by our hitting, or even our pitching, since we had David Price and Rick Porcello at the top of the rotation. The bigger surprise was Price. He was the man. I didn't know him that well before we had our problems on the field. It had been a respectful relationship, but not a deep one. After he'd hit me with a pitch in 2014, neither one of us was trying to be buddies. But having the chance to see Price every day changed my perspective. I can tell you that he's one of the best teammates I've ever had. He's the kind of person you want to be around. He goes above and beyond to make his teammates feel comfortable, whether it's giving us shoes — as he did multiple times during the season — or bringing in a caterer. Or just having a connection with everyone, making sure we're all right.

In his first 10 to 12 starts, he wasn't shutting hitters down the way he usually did, but I liked what I heard. Or what I didn't hear. He didn't make excuses, and he never ran away from his problems. Once I saw that was the way he handled himself, no matter what his performance was, I knew he would be one of the free agents who makes it in Boston.

At every stop of the season, at least three or four times a day, someone would ask, "Are you sure you want to retire?" I'd smile at the question and be respectful, but the answer was always the same. Yes, I was 100 percent sure. Before making my decision, I'd talked to numerous people. One of them, of course, was my father. He didn't even need to hear my explanation. He said he understood.

I was so thankful to be in the position to retire at 40 rather than, say, 65, and my father was a big reason that was possible. As hard as I worked at baseball, I never came close to working as hard as my parents. My dad was at work six days a week. He didn't see me play a lot of my games when I was growing up because he was working, trying to make sure we had what we needed. He was a great father and a no-nonsense one as well. I did my work and stayed out of trouble because I respected him so much and didn't want to disappoint him. He was the one who kept pushing me toward baseball and telling me that I had a gift for the game. To be able to retire as a good player, and have my father alive to see his dream realized, was meaningful to me.

I'd also talked with John Henry before making the decision. He asked me if I was sure and I assured him that I was. His response was that the organization would have my back the entire way. I thought of all the things I'd been through and how upset and embarrassed I'd been when the Twins released me. Then I thought about what it meant that I had landed in a historic franchise, in a city with my same spirit, playing for an owner who wanted to win. Just because you have the money to own a baseball team doesn't mean you're guaranteed to love the game. Mr. Henry loves the game, and I could feel how much he appreciated me as a player. That meant a lot to me. I did not always agree with the Red Sox, and we had our conflicts over money, but that was business. Always has been and always will be. As I went through the season, I made myself pause every now and then and just think about how truly fortunate I had been.

I played for 20 seasons. Do you realize how many bad things *could* have happened over 20 years? I remember one year we had an ordeal in Cleveland. The airplane went damn near sideways. We were supposed to touch down in Cleveland's international airport, but we wound up going back up and making plans for landing at a private airport. We were freaking out.

Guys were legitimately scared. I was sitting next to one of our relievers at the time, Bobby Jenks. He turned to me with total fear and sincerity and said, "Papi, don't worry. God will take care of our families."

That's how bad it was.

Let's be real and honest. There are so many challenges and temptations that can affect your personal life when you have spent 20 years in the big leagues. You don't know who you can trust. We spend a lot of time on the road by ourselves. You have to be careful about the people you allow into your life and get clear about their intentions and expectations. You never know who can play a trick on you. It happens with a lot of players. There are beautiful women in every city, and many opportunities to meet up with them. Sometimes it's harmless. Sometimes it's a case of someone seeking attention, or more. Even innocent situations can become tricky.

I remember once being driven out of Fenway after a game, and a crowd had gathered around my car as we tried turning onto Yawkey Way. I signed several autographs, but then many fans began to overwhelm the car. I stopped signing and drove away. Later, I heard that a fan wanted to sue because apparently part of one of the wheels hit his foot. After that, I came up with a new rule: never sign autographs in the car. Look, it's a challenge, man. Being a famous athlete has its price. You put up with a lot of shit that people don't see or understand. Being in a position to come out of those 20 years with my reputation intact has been a blessing.

I was more than happy to share my wisdom with young players on our team, or any other team. I didn't want to see anyone get caught up in something avoidable. One thing I learned early on is that some people out there want to misinterpret the message. So one of my rules was to never take a picture with someone holding a drink, unless it was obvious that it was in a place where many people were drinking. Another thing I wouldn't do was take a picture on an elevator or in a hotel room. The world can be twisted at times, and some people will try to say or do anything for some money.

As I got ready for my 10th and final All-Star Game, in San Diego, I reflected on how fortunate I was to be honored there. No one thought that would be the case in 2009. They expected me to be out of the game, not hitting .332 with 22 home runs. In 2009, when the *New York Times* story accusing me of doping came out, I had been to five All-Star Games, and the thought was that I wouldn't be going to any more. I was now at my fifth one since being accused. I was still hitting. Still relevant. But that wasn't even the biggest victory for me. It was talking to the commissioner, Rob Manfred, and hearing him say that the list I was on in 2003 was not proof of any performance-enhancing drug violation. That supported what I'd been saying for years! It was gratifying to hear that from him after I'd experienced years of blatant and subtle attacks on my legitimacy.

It had reached an all-time level of silliness in 2014, when I was approaching 500 career home runs. I would get drug-tested for a night game, then again for the day game the next day. They would test me on the road, and again four days later at home. With random testing, being tested four or five times in a month was unheard of. The typical player might be tested two or three times in a season. Not me. I was being tested at an extraordinary rate because that old story had put doubt and confusion in everyone's heads. I used to get mad at every joker saying something in print, on TV, talk radio, or Twitter, or at the park. But as my career started coming to an end, I decided to view the tests as a challenge. As motivation. I wanted as many tests as possible so there would be no excuses later. It got to the point where I'd see the drug-testing guy coming in and say to him, "I'm ready. Let's go."

In the final two months of the season, a few things were clear to me. One was that I was going to love watching the Red Sox once I retired. Porcello and Price are both aces, and Porcello was having the best season of his career. The young players who had been with the team since April had all become All-Stars. And when we got into August, the franchise called up its first-round pick from 2014, an outfielder named Andrew Benintendi. He'd risen quickly through the season, and it was easy to see why. For a young player, he had a strong understanding of the strike zone and hitting. I made sure his locker was right next to mine.

I was also humbled by the kind words and gifts from other teams. They gave me paintings, wine, barbecue sauce, cowboy boots, and even a gag gift — the Twins gave me peanut butter, a reminder of the time Corey Koskie pranked me with peanut butter in my underwear. I would have appreciated these gifts and tributes from other teams even if we hadn't been winning, but being in the playoff mix after having no chance the previous two years made it sweeter.

Just after Labor Day, we took over first place in the division and held on to it for the rest of the season. I looked at our team, and the competition, and I didn't see any reason why we couldn't win the World Series. Honestly, I thought we were the best team in baseball.

I was surprised at how much I stayed balanced, maintaining my normal level of production at the plate, while every day, no matter where I went, someone wanted a piece of me. I'm not exaggerating. I was asked for something every day of the season. Even our neighbors, who we're friendly with, noticed it and became very protective of us. They'd see a film crew outside and immediately wonder if it was authorized. They would call and ask us, "Is that paparazzi out there?" Another time we got an early morning phone call. "Hey, someone is climbing your fence." The fence was broken, and it was simply a repairman coming to fix it. Another time, one of our neighbors was unaware that the police escort I'd had to Gillette Stadium in mid-September to be honored by the Patriots was a special occasion, and she became concerned that I'd have to travel like that at all times for the rest of the season.

Maybe my neighbors knew I was wearing down before I knew it myself. I could feel it a bit during our last road trip of the season, at Yankee Stadium. I loved New York and respected everything about the Yankees. But I desperately wanted to sweep them as part of my New York good-bye.

I'd made a lot of memories there, both the kind that most baseball fans had seen on TV and a few that happened on team buses and planes and were preserved on video. I might even be the only one who has those videos. Once, as part of hazing the rookies, we made them dress in women's clothing. We had guys in fishnet stockings and wigs, players in cheerleading miniskirts and dresses. Once we got to New York and were on the team bus to the hotel, we made a detour to Broadway. We asked the rookies to get out and dance as yours truly hummed the melody to "New York, New York."

Those are some of the things I will never forget . . . or delete. My last trip to New York was less joyful, more reflective, probably because of all I had on my mind. Despite clinching the division there, it was frustrating to be getting swept in the series. It was New York. It's in my blood to want to beat the Yankees, and I was pissed that we didn't. But I was blown away by what I felt was the most thoughtful farewell gift of them all.

It was such a contrast between Baltimore and New York. I had destroyed a Camden Yards phone with my bat after being ejected from a game in 2013. So, in a move that had Buck Showalter written all over it, the Orioles gave me a phone as a retirement present. A couple of my boys on the Orioles, Chris Davis and Adam Jones, apologized for it while we were on the field. I played along and smiled, but it took a lot of restraint not to just walk away and turn my back on their "humor."

But New York, as usual, set the standard. The Yankees always seemed to find the most appropriate way to celebrate their own players and, in some cases, the competition. That organization was a big part of my story. I didn't know how much harder I had to work until I got to Boston, and I didn't know how much I craved winning until I'd lost to the Yankees in 2003. I had noticed that not only did they win, but they expected to win. It was an attitude that they had and we needed to develop, no matter what the history of the Red Sox had been.

It was a pleasure to be a part of baseball history and to compete against men like Derek Jeter, Mariano Rivera, Jorge Posada, Andy Pettitte, Gary Sheffield, Tino Martinez, and even the managers, Joe Torre and Joe Girardi. There were so many memories that I couldn't put into words, so I was speechless when the Yankees did exactly that. They presented me with a leather-bound album with handwritten letters from several players, describing what it was like for them to compete against me. It was overwhelming, and truly one of the best gifts, of any kind, that I'd ever received.

By the time I got back to Boston, I was worn out. I'm not going to lie about it. The last few days of the regular season, I was dragging. It was the accumulation of events, the schedule, and age. I felt every part of someone who was almost 41 years old and still playing baseball.

What distracted me from the fatigue was the generosity and thoughtfulness of the Red Sox. They know how to put on a celebration, and they came up with one of their best in the final weekend.

My father, my sister, my wife, and my children were there. My former teammates were there. Danilo Medina, the president of the Dominican Republic, kept a promise he had made to me in February and was in attendance. The governor of Massachusetts, Charlie Baker, and the mayor of Boston, Marty Walsh, both made presentations.

I looked at it all and didn't even think of myself. I was hopeful that the story, my story, could inspire someone who needed to believe in turnarounds and transformations.

Unfortunately, the story didn't end the way I was sure that it would. The retirement tour had been so much about my past, so it was fitting that two names from my past blocked us in the playoffs. We played the Cleveland Indians, who had Tito Francona as their manager and Andrew Miller as their key pitching weapon. My mentality the whole year had been to win the World Series. I never thought for a second that the Indians could beat us.

I also hadn't given Tito enough credit. He probably would never admit it, but our team was better than his. But I saw him do something the entire series that blew my mind. As soon as he got a lead, he started thinking about bringing Miller into the game. He got a lead three times, and he went with that formula three times.

Tito was more aggressive than I'd ever seen him. That's what the playoffs are all about, aggression in a short series, and he tipped the series with Miller. We had a lot, but we didn't have him. Miller was just filthy. He's the kind of pitcher who can play games with lefties and righties. He can make right-handed hitters look like shit. And when a left-handed pitcher can make a righty look bad, that means lefties have no chance. The guy is six-seven and he throws it 99 miles per hour. He also has a huge, devastating slider. His release point totally fucks you up. You don't see where the ball is coming from. What do I see when I face him? I don't see anything.

When we left Cleveland down 0–2, a lot of people asked me if

I'd given any thought to the final game of my career. I hadn't. I was convinced that we were going to come back and win the series. We'd done it before.

Their starting pitcher for Game 3 was Josh Tomlin. I had faced him many times. I had hit the ball hard against him, homered off him, seen the ball well with no problems against him. But that night he was the best I had ever seen him. I kept waiting for his mistakes and he didn't make them. That's baseball. Sometimes the pitchers get you, and sometimes you get them.

It's life too, and I was emotional for the first time in a long time. It was time to start my life after baseball. I hadn't given it the thought it deserved, because I was convinced that I would give my farewell speech as I held another World Series trophy.

Instead, I went back to the small and painfully quiet clubhouse with my teammates. John Farrell spoke first. He told us that we'd had an incredible year. He should have said the same for himself. He'd beaten cancer and taken a team from last place to first. Managing in Boston, in this division, is a bitch. My boy Kevin Cash had dark hair when he became manager in Tampa and the job turned his whole head gray. This is not a PlayStation game. It's a hard job.

I spoke next and thanked everyone for the year, and the support. I let them know that I was their brother, and I was here for them if they needed me. Hanley Ramírez choked me up a bit when he told me that it had been an honor to play with me.

The tears flowed down my cheeks as I walked those stairs from the dugout to the field, one last time. I went to the mound and raised my cap to all the fans who remained. They were my brothers and sisters too. For 14 years, they had encouraged me more than they ever knew with their passion, their cheers, and even their tears.

After I woke up the next morning, I sat in my family room, where a thick book rested on the coffee table. It was the album from the

Yankees, and I paged through it. Joe Torre joked that he wished I'd retired in 2003. Jorge Posada, in perfect handwritten Spanish, said that I was a friend and brother. Joe Girardi talked about baseball, but said he was more impressed with the way I stood up for the city of Boston in 2013. They were all beautiful sentiments, including the one from Derek Jeter, who spoke to the new chapter in my life. Jeter wrote that I'd had a great career, with awards, championships, and hard work. But now, he wrote, "it's time for you to relax."

Acknowledgments

Fourteen years ago, I never imagined I'd be able to write a book like this.

I was new to the Red Sox and New England in 2003, and I'd be exaggerating if I claimed that thousands of people were watching my every move. They weren't. No one knew what a Big Papi was, because that nickname hadn't even been born yet. I was simply "David Ortiz," or "the new guy who used to play for the Twins." Outside of my relatives, along with Pedro Martinez and Manny Ramirez, there weren't many who thought I could help deliver a long-awaited World Series title to Boston. But to be a part of three? Not even Pedro or Manny predicted that. Neither did I.

From the moment I decided that 2016 would be my final season, I knew I wanted to make sure I was able to tell my story. For my entire career, much has been written about me. Some of the stories were glowing pieces about my relationship with Boston and baseball. Others called for me to retire long before the final season, including a media suggestion from early 2010: "Stick a fork in him." I knew as I entered retirement I'd have an opportunity to talk directly to you and tell you the most accurate account of my career. I'm truly blessed to have had such a gratifying life in baseball, and I'm hopeful that you all enjoyed coming along for the ride. It's been a tremendous journey and it wouldn't have been possible without the help of hundreds of people, some of whom I'll name here (and many others who helped in ways, large and small, over the course of 20 big-league seasons).

I want to especially thank everyone in Boston and all of New England. Boston has inspired me in so many ways, and I hope I offered it a fraction of what it gave my family and me. To the entire Red Sox organization, specifically team owners John Henry and Tom Werner, thank you for reviving and establishing my career in this legendary organization. You were thoughtful each day of my final season; it will be a year of my life that I'll never forget. To my teammates, past and present, you guys are the ones who made it easy to go to work every day. The moments we've shared together, from pranks to profound conversations, give us a brotherly bond that will always be a part of me. I wouldn't be in Boston without Pedro, and I wouldn't have known so much about hitting without Manny. My deepest gratitude to them, and others, for a variety of reasons: Mariano Rivera, Hanley Ramírez, Robinson Cano, Adam Jones, Torii Hunter, Dustin Pedroia, Mike Trout, Mookie Betts, Jonny Gomes, Jon Lester, David Price, Brad Radke, Corey Koskie, Doug Mientkiewicz, Sean Casey, Kevin Millar, Xander Bogaerts, Jackie Bradley Jr. To all the baseball fans around the country, thank you for the love you showed on the road for the majority of my Red Sox career, and in an incredibly generous way in 2016. Who would have ever thought that Big Papi chants would break out nationally, even in Yankee Stadium!

To everyone in my home country, the beautiful Dominican Republic, I'm so proud to represent our people. One of the most flattering, and humbling, moments was seeing the largest Dominican flag ever displayed outside of the country at Fenway during my final game. I never imagined that I'd have a life like this, but now that I have it, my intention is not to just accumulate things for myself. I consider it part of my mission to do everything in my power to use God's blessings to better the lives of as many people as I can in the Dominican, through the David Ortiz Children's Fund.

It would likely take a few hundred more pages to properly credit my family. Let me try to say it this way to my wife, Tiffany, and my kids, Jessica, Alex, and D'Angelo: Thank you for always being there for me, no matter what the circumstance. I lived the unusual and demanding baseball life for two decades, and you all made supporting me look so easy. I know it wasn't, and I'm grateful for your love and understanding (I'll be able to make more games, school concerts, and impromptu weekend trips now).

My father, Leo, has been my biggest role model and supporter. Thank you, Pop, for making me into the man that I am today. My mother, Angela, is my guardian angel. I know she's been watching over me since she physically left the world in 2002. Mom, I hope your baby boy made you smile with every heavenward point as I crossed home plate.

I have a smart and diligent management team behind me, and it's their planning and foresight that allowed me to relax and focus on playing the game. From my first days in Boston, my marketing agent Alex Radetsky has been right by my side. This project wouldn't be possible without him and his entire group at Radegen Sports Management, including Angelo Solomita, Michael Lecce, Jennifer Cronin, and Alexis Walberg. I'm also grateful for my longtime agents, Fernando Cuza and Diego Bentz; my financial adviser, Mark Walker; and my good friend Jose Luis, who has been like a second father to my kids and a brother to me. I can't thank you enough for how you've looked out for my family.

I'm indebted to several people at Houghton Mifflin Harcourt. The staff there clearly has a commitment to telling good stories, and I'm happy that mine is now a part of the impressive list. Thanks to editor

Susan Canavan for her intelligence and skill, making sure that the stories that readers most wanted to hear made it to these pages in a compelling way. Megan Wilson, Hannah Harlow, Jenny Xu, and Beth Burleigh Fuller were also instrumental in putting things together. My coauthor, Michael Holley, was the perfect person to help tell this story. We had hours upon hours of meaningful conversations, which led to this book, the most honest representation of who I am. Thanks also to the Red Sox for providing photos of some of the most memorable moments in my career.

Appendix
CAREER STATISTICS

David Ortiz

BORN: November 18, 1975, in Santo Domingo, Dominican Republic

HEIGHT: 6'4"

WEIGHT: 240 lbs.

BATS: Left

SIGNED: Seattle Mariners, 1992

MAJOR LEAGUE BASEBALL DEBUT: Minnesota Twins, 1997

SIGNED AS FREE AGENT: Boston Red Sox, December 2002

10-TIME ALL-STAR, 7-TIME SILVER SLUGGER, 3-TIME WORLD SERIES CHAMPION, WORLD SERIES MVP, 541 HR (17th in MLB history)

MAJOR LEAGUE STATISTICS

YEAR	TEAM	G	AB	R	H	2B	3B	HR	RBI	BB	AVG	OBP	SLG
1997	MIN	15	49	10	16	3	0	1	6	2	.327	.353	.449
1998	MIN	86	278	47	77	20	0	9	46	39	.277	.371	.446
1999	MIN	10	20	1	0	0	0	0	0	5	.000	.200	.000
2000	MIN	130	415	59	117	36	1	10	63	57	.282	.364	.446
2001	MIN	89	303	46	71	17	1	18	48	40	.234	.324	.475
2002	MIN	125	412	52	112	32	1	20	75	43	.272	.339	.500
2003	BOS	128	448	79	129	39	2	31	101	58	.288	.369	.592
2004	BOS	150	582	94	175	47	3	41	139	75	.301	.380	.603
2005	BOS	159	601	119	180	40	1	47	148	102	.300	.397	.604
2006	BOS	151	558	115	160	29	2	54	137	119	.287	.413	.636
2007	BOS	149	549	116	182	52	1	35	117	111	.332	.445	.621
2008	BOS	109	416	74	110	30	1	23	89	70	.264	.369	.507
2009	BOS	150	541	77	129	35	1	28	99	74	.238	.332	.462
2010	BOS	145	518	86	140	36	1	32	102	82	.270	.370	.529

YEAR	TEAM	G	AB	R	H	2B	3B	HR	RBI	BB	AVG	OBP	SLG
2011	BOS	146	525	84	162	40	1	29	96	78	.309	.398	.554
2012	BOS	90	324	65	103	26	0	23	60	56	.318	.415	.611
2013	BOS	137	518	84	160	38	2	30	103	76	.309	.395	.564
2014	BOS	142	518	59	136	27	0	35	104	75	.263	.355	.517
2015	BOS	146	528	73	144	37	0	37	108	77	.273	.360	.553
2016	BOS	151	537	79	169	48	1	38	127	80	.315	.401	.020

KEY

G = Games

AB = At Bats

R = Runs

H = Hits

2B = Doubles

3B = Triples

HR = Home Runs

RBI = Runs Batted In

BB = Walks

AVG = Batting Average

OBP = On Base Percentage

SLG = Slugging Percentage

Index